Mentoring in the
Early Years

Mentoring in the
Early Years

Edited by
Alison Robins

P·C·P
Paul Chapman
Publishing

 P·CP

Paul Chapman Publishing
A SAGE Publications company
1 Oliver's Yard
55 City Road
London EC1Y 1SP

SAGE Publications Inc
2455 Teller Road
Thousand Oaks
California 91320

SAGE Publications India Pvt Ltd
B 1/I 1 Mohan Cooperative Industrial Area
Mathura Road, New Delhi 110 044
India

SAGE Publications Asia-Pacific Pte Ltd
33 Pekin Street #02-01
Far East Square
Singapore 048763

Library of Congress Control Number: 2006925185

A catalogue record for this book is available from the British Library

ISBN 978-1-4129-2235-7
ISBN 978-1-4129-2236-4 (pbk)

Typeset by Pantek Arts Ltd, Maidstone, Kent
Printed in Great Britain by TJ International, Padstow, Cornwall
Printed on paper from sustainable resources

Contents

About the contributors

Sue Callan has been a member of the collaborative partnership team for the Foundation Degree in Early years at the University of Worcester for three years. She was course manager for the programme at Evesham College and is now responsible, as a member of the UW Centre for Early Childhood team, within the Institute of Education, for its delivery through Herefordshire EYDCP. Sue has been an adult education tutor for fifteen years, specialising in community-based pre-school practice and working with mature students in both personal tutor and mentor roles.

Eryl Copp is course leader and manager of professional practice in early years at Worcester College of Technology. She is a mentor tutor and personal tutor for the Foundation Degree in Early Years. Eryl has taught in primary and nursery schools and has been a nursery school head teacher and external assessor.

Victoria Eadie is team leader and manager for the Foundation Degree in Early Years and Foundation Degree in Learning Support at Josiah Mason College, Birmingham. She manages the tutor and practice mentor team for both courses and is a personal tutor for both cohorts of students. Vicki has also taught on early years courses such as DCE and NVQ and has written and delivered short courses on Birth to Three Matters, Behaviour Management and Child Protection.

Kate Fowler is a senior lecturer in the Centre for Early Childhood team within the Institute of Education at the University of Worcester. Kate has taught in nursery, primary and middle schools. She has been a link tutor supporting teacher mentors of Initial Teacher Education students studying PGCE and BA QTS at UW.

Sarah Kelly has worked part-time for the past ten years at the Centre for Research in Early Childhood within the Institute of Education at the University of Worcester as a trainer and early years adviser for the Effective Early Learning Programme. She is a practice mentor for the Foundation Degree in Early Years working with students from Josiah Mason College, Birmingham, and

Herefordshire EYDCP. Sarah also runs a toy and resource library for a rural SureStart project in Herefordshire.

Janet Murray is a principal lecturer and Head of the Centre for Early Childhood within the Institute of Education at the University of Worcester. She led the initial development and validation of the SureStart-recognised Sector-endorsed Foundation Degree in Early Years at UW, which incorporates a unique tiered system of mentoring support. Janet has taught in and managed early years provision in both the maintained and non-maintained sectors in the UK and abroad.

Melanie Pilcher is an early years trainer and part-time lecturer at Evesham College. She is also the Staff Support Co-ordinator for Worcestershire NHS and is nearing completion of an MA (Educational Management). Melanie is a practice mentor for the Foundation Degree in Early Years and has worked closely with the UW partner institutions to develop a support package for practice mentors and induction materials for new mentors.

Alison Robins is a senior lecturer in the Centre for Early Childhood Team within the Institute of Education at the University of Worcester. She is the co-ordinator of the Foundation Degree in Early Years and was involved in the development and validation of the degree, which runs at six partner institutions. Alison has taught in primary and middle schools, has been a SENCO and deputy head and has worked as a Teaching Assistant Training Officer for Worcestershire Local Authority.

Acknowledgements

The editor would like to acknowledge the contribution of all the authors within this book. It is a project that has been undertaken when work commitments just seem to get busier and busier and it is therefore a credit to everyone's professionalism and passion for the field within which they all work that we have achieved our aim. Thanks must also go to Jude Bowen and Charlotte Saunders at Sage publications for their enthusiasm and assistance throughout this project.

On a personal level I believe that the impetus for this book came from a much wider team of colleagues who have, for the last three years, been completely dedicated to providing quality experiences for all the students undertaking the Foundation Degree in Early Years at a number of the University of Worcester's partner institutions. I would like to thank them all for their support and hard work.

We would also like to thank the staff, children and parents at South Worcestershire Primary Care Trust's Noah's Ark Day Nursery (see the frontispiece), for allowing us to take the photographs used in this book and John Lusardi for his photographic skills.

As a text we hope this book will be of benefit to the dedicated and highly motivated early years professionals for whom it is written.

Alison Robins

Introduction
Alison Robins

Most of us have an inbuilt desire to learn and also to help others in learning. These desires have been described by Clutterbuck (2004: 3) as 'deep seated emotional drives within most people'. He goes on to say how the human instinct that leads us to pass on information, knowledge and wisdom to others goes hand in hand with the ability also to receive it. However, he then provides us with somewhat of a warning:

> It often occurs that the desire of the more experienced person (especially if he or she is much older) to pass on accumulated wisdom exceeds greatly the desire of the less experienced person to listen. Most people may have the instinct to be a mentor, but to do the role well requires a capacity to hold back and allow people to learn for themselves.
>
> (2004: 3)

As professionals working within the field of early years we are aware of the fundamental principles within our practice that underpin early learning. These principles include the notions that:

- Children develop at different rates, and in different ways.
- All children have abilities which can (and should be) identified and promoted.
- Young children should learn from everything that happens to them and around them.
- Children learn most effectively through actions, rather than from instruction.
- Children learn best when they are actively involved and interested.
- Children who feel confident in themselves and their own ability have a head start to learning.
- Children need time and space to produce work of quality and depth.
- Play and conversation are the main ways by which young children learn about themselves, other people and the world around them.

- Children who are encouraged to think for themselves are more likely to act independently.
- The relationships which children make with other children and with adults are of central importance to their development.

(Ball, cited in Drury *et al.*, 2000: 17).

Reflecting upon these principles, and considering the role we play in 'mentoring' the children within our settings, is it not the case that they could be applied equally to the learning that takes place for practitioners being supported by a mentor?

This book was written as a result of being involved in the development of the SureStart-recognised Sector-endorsed Foundation Degree in Early Years (FdA EY) at the University of Worcester (UW) and the need expressed at the National Network for the Early Years Foundation Degrees for guidance and advice when mentoring students undertaking this programme.

Mentoring is regarded as an important part of good professional practice and is well established within the field of primary and secondary education. Consequently, the majority of texts available on this topic are written very much with a focus on schools and colleges.

This text has a wider audience and is aimed at early years settings. In these mentoring takes place constantly and the role is undertaken by many different people and involves many varied partnerships. For example, nursery managers will mentor new employees or students undertaking practice experience; Higher Level Teaching Assistants (HLTAs) mentor fellow Teaching Assistants (TAs); teachers mentor newly qualified teachers (NQTs) and colleagues mentor each other in order to evaluate and develop practice within their workplace. Accordingly, this book will aim to serve the needs of the diverse 'types' of mentors within early years settings.

With such a broad audience and, following much consideration and debate between the author team, it was decided that, unless otherwise stated and justified, the terms 'mentor' and 'practitioner' would be used throughout.

The government agenda associated with the Children's Workforce Strategy (DfES, 2006) emphasises the need for specialised help in order to promote opportunity, prevent problems and act early if and when problems arise. This can be associated with the staff working within the sector and also the children and families with whom we work in partnership. From whichever perspective we consider this, trained professionals are essential to the process and the government also acknowledges the need for recognised standards and accredited qualifications within the sector. With the onus on settings to demonstrate high standards and quality in all areas, and an increasing number of qualifications, such as foundation degrees, being work-based in nature, the role of the mentor is of utmost importance.

The aim of the book

The aim of this book is to provide practical guidance for professionals undertaking mentoring, giving advice on how to carry out this role effectively. The chapters provide the reader with a mixture of relevant theory, practical suggestions, case studies, questions for reflection and discussion (pauses for thought), activities for professional development and suggestions for further reading. There are materials and suggestions within the book that may be copied and used as appropriate. The topics covered can be considered individually or together with other chapters.

Children enjoying play and conversation

Content

Chapter 1 acknowledges current models of mentoring practice with a view to identifying a framework for mentoring in the context of early years. It challenges mentors to reflect on the complex nature of their role in order to promote a clearer awareness of its significance to quality in training, practice and delivery of services to young children and their families. Chapter 2 explores the complexity of relationships within the mentor role, gives top tips to support the development of these relationships and provides working examples and scenarios that consider what may be done when things 'go wrong'. Reflective practice is fundamental to improving quality within early years settings, ourselves and those we mentor as practitioners and lifelong learners. This notion is discussed in Chapter 3 and practical suggestions are offered for how the reflective process may be taught. The development of some form of portfolio of evidence is a goal for many practitioners being supported by a mentor. Chapter 4 takes the mentor and practitioner through a profiling exercise from beginning to end, identifying challenges along the way and offering strategies for overcoming potential problems. Chapter 5 is based upon an active mentoring scheme and identifies the principles underpinning the design of the mentoring scheme for early years practitioners seeking Senior Practitioner Status through the SureStart-recognised Sector-endorsed Foundation Degree in Early Years. The final chapter is a case study which takes the reader through a journey which involved a mentor supporting the process of change. It considers the effectiveness and outcomes of having a mentor working alongside practitioners to reflect upon, develop and improve the quality of experience for young children.

1

What is mentoring?

Sue Callan

This chapter will explain the role of the mentor. It will look at current models of mentoring, and will identify a framework for mentoring in the context of early years values, traditions and emerging social policy. This chapter will identify some of the structures that need to be in place to ensure effective practice. Overall, the aim is to allow mentors in early years to gain an understanding of the complex nature of their role and its significance to quality in training, practice and delivery of services to young children and their families. 'Pause for thought' boxes are provided to raise issues that are developed as practical strategies in subsequent chapters.

Terminology

In this chapter the terms 'mentor' and 'practitioner' are used to cover all possible contexts. 'Mentor' is role-specific in that it will apply to all those in formal 'advisory' relationships with practitioners. As 'practitioners' will not necessarily be students in the formal sense of the term, but will usually be based in early years settings, this term is chosen to reflect the work-based situation. 'Manager' in this chapter refers to those who are responsible for the organisation of mentoring, for example a course leader or workplace manager.

The evolution of mentoring and current practices

The role of mentor is recognised across all areas of society. From the responsibility accepted by Mentor for the son of Odysseus in Greek mythology, through the pre-industrial guilds and later apprenticeships in industrial trades, the idea of a more experienced individual assisting the transmission of knowledge and skills has become culturally embedded. The corporate business world has developed systems of mentoring which are integral to the induction and supported development of new company employees. In recent years such practices have spread to the wider community. There are programmes in schools and universities for peer/pupil mentoring, church and youth organisations, parent support (through organisations such as Home Start as well as other voluntary self-help groups), access to employment programmes, mentoring as part of commitment to promoting diversity and overcoming barriers to inclusion – among other examples.

In the field of initial teacher training, Qualified Teacher Status (QTS) induction programmes and continuing professional development, mentoring is highly significant within both training institutes and schools. Understanding the process in education has become more refined as a result of action research, such as that undertaken by Furlong and Maynard (1995) and more recent DFES-sponsored studies (www.teachernet.gov.uk/docbank) which are noted in Chapter 3. As a result school-based practice mentors have many resources to draw on, with national guidance expected to be published in the near future. However, developments in early education and the breadth of provision in the early years sector have resulted in the use of mentoring across conventional professional contexts – for example, the use of visiting teachers as practice mentors in community pre-schools and private day nurseries, reflecting the integration of services and multi-disciplinary work within the field.

An understanding of mentoring and the development of practice does not occur in isolation from organisational or national culture. Similarly, mentoring systems should draw on best practice from a range of models and clarity of definition regarding purpose, expectation and specific context is important to the success of such schemes. This chapter explores these themes with a view to establishing some common principles for the early years.

Policy framework for early years practice

Mentoring practice in the early years has not evolved in a vacuum. Just as colleagues involved in teacher training have adjusted training programmes to accommodate political ideology, government policy objectives for teacher training and funding issues in higher educational establishments, similar external pressures are brought to bear in early years settings.

Early years mentors need to be aware of the social and political context in which they operate. Few practitioners within the sector will deny that the years since 1990 have transformed the status of early years services and education in the United Kingdom. Indeed, taking a slightly longer perspective, change has been an evolving process from the mid-1980s – the 1989 Education Act being identified as one influence for much of what has followed for early years education under both Conservative and Labour agendas.

The key principles underpinning policy under the National Childcare Strategy (DfES, 1997) include partnership, integrated services, continuity and

Informal discussion between mentor and practitioner

progression for children in all services (from birth to age nineteen as the result of *Every Child Matters* (DfES, 2004) and the 2004 Children Act), inclusion and quality in the full breadth of practice. In concrete terms policy has encompassed a range of measures such as the Curriculum Guidance for the Foundation Stage, Birth to Three Matters, Children's Centres, Early Years Development and Childcare Partnerships (EYDCP), the DfES/QCA Training Framework and Common Core of Knowledge for practitioners – demonstrating links and progression through to the competence-based model of the Teacher Training Agency. The Work Force Strategy (DfES, 2006) and remodelling of the role of teachers and teaching assistants in schools also impacts on practitioners in the Foundation Stage as does the changing role of schools in the community under the extended schools projects. Most significant is the debate about the 'new practitioner', developments in our understanding of the adult role in these integrated services and more recent moves toward a 'birth to five' progressive framework (Early Years Foundation Stage) for children's early development and learning.

In such a context the role of the mentor has increased in importance and complexity, especially as work-based training is an established element of vocational qualifications as well as academic programmes across further and higher education. One example is the SureStart-recognised Sector-endorsed Foundation Degree in Early Years (FdA EY) which incorporates a substantial mentoring component, the aim of which is to encourage practitioners to go beyond a minimum level of competence and encourage reflective practice.

In order to clarify the features of mentoring for those involved in the early years, it will be useful to progress discussion in terms of first principles for the role of the mentor. Subsequent chapters will build on these key issues, providing techniques and strategies for meeting the challenges of the role.

Common themes in theory and practice: role and qualities of the mentor

One part of the mentor role has been identified with reference to the policy framework. The mentor assists in the transmission of knowledge and skills and encourages practitioners to develop reflective practice. In this respect, the mentor is a 'bridge' between the academic forum and the day-to-day experience encountered by practitioners in early years settings. Most important, the mentor promotes reflection, because this develops the confidence and competence of individual practitioners working with the theories, principles and philosophy of the early years sector.

Whilst the role will be common to all contexts, mentors will take account of the fact that student practitioners are not always young and/or inexperienced. For example, a requirement of the FdA EY is that students are established practitioners with at least two years' post-qualification experience. Similarly, in business practice, experienced professionals may be assigned a mentor to help with focus on a new range of skills or specific responsibilities. The relatively new professional and management qualifications in school headship and integrated centre leadership reflect the emerging emphasis on ongoing professional development for managers in early years settings. As a result, there is a mentor function within these programmes.

It is recognised that the usefulness of mentoring in terms of *continuing* professional development has become an accepted justification for mentoring practice and is consistent with the fact that practitioners in the workplace also contribute to training through such 'in-house' variations as professional critical friend or the formalised mentor teacher schemes initiated through local authorities.

With these general themes in mind the remainder of this chapter will concentrate on practical definition of the mentoring role for early years, the qualities of the mentor and the value base for good mentoring practice.

A mentor in early years

Dictionary definitions suggest that mentoring has something to do with passing on wisdom. In a well established guide to mentoring, Clutterbuck (2004) notes that such general understandings are too vague to be helpful, as they lead to confusion with other similar roles such as coaching or buddying systems.

In developing a clearer definition, Wilkin (1992) argues that the role of the mentor should be framed in relation to specific frameworks, such as training or qualification requirements. This approach provides a principle that can be broadly applied to early years contexts. If we accept that the framework within which both mentor and practitioner operate is determined by the 'curriculum' for the child and the vision of the professional practitioner within it, then it is possible to propose a more specific definition for mentoring.

The mentor will help practitioners find answers to challenging situations, assist with strategies for action in the job role, promote both nurture and challenge within the boundaries of the relationship with the practitioner and encourage sustained motivation in the work place. The mentor in the early years will therefore work within a role defined by the requirements of the philosophical and political tradition outlined above. This in turn suggests a set of qualities and a philosophy of mentoring with which to develop the early years model.

PAUSE FOR THOUGHT

Who are the people who have influenced you in your personal and professional development as an early years practitioner? Why were they so influential? Are there common characteristics that they share?

Qualities of the 'ideal' mentor

Good humour, enthusiastic, inspirational, problem solver, supportive, knowledgeable and competent in subject skills and practices, creative thinker, good communication and interpersonal skills, good partner skills, able to resolve or defuse conflict, effective time manager, prioritises and sets targets, action plans, report writing, 'politically' astute beyond the immediate context, reflective.

To be fair, such perfectly formed individuals may not exist and the importance of ongoing training and professional development for mentors must be an accepted part of good practice. However, Pegg (2000) notes that such qualities provide mentors with credibility for the role. Underpinning this skill set is the fact that mentors will be/have been successful practitioners in their own right and be recognised as 'streetwise' in this respect in order to encourage evaluation and reflection in the practitioner. The particular mix of qualities will also enable the mentor to bring realistic expectations and a sense of proportion to a role which is complex and can be challenging at times.

In line with other models of mentoring, the early years mentor will inevitably combine these qualities with a mix of approaches and strategies – adviser, teacher, buddy, guide, coach, facilitator, counsellor, role model and leader. Clutterbuck (2004) suggests that these each have distinct purposes, and as specific activities they are further explored below.

Early years: values and principles for mentoring

In addition to these personal and professional qualities, mentors in the early years will have a philosophy of mentoring and training that also fits with the traditions of the sector. Many practitioners will recognise the concept of 'scaffolding' for learning and development from early years theoretical approaches. Just as this sets the qualitative framework for work with children, the mentor will be similarly consistent in applying underpinning beliefs and strategies with regard to adult interactions. The way in which the mentor role is conducted in early years practice will set the tone for the experience and outcomes for the practitioner. Clutterbuck (2004) explains mentoring as providing the 'reflective space' in the teaching and learning spectrum – the mentor poses questions and uses discussion in order to enable the building of 'wisdom'. Mentoring serves the practitioner in that it encourages, empowers and enhances a continuing commitment to experiential learning at the heart of work-based practice and offers the possibility of change. The guidance offered by the mentor is carried out in the spirit of mutual respect, where power is shared as far as the situation allows, and there is an expectation of two-way learning. Both mentor and practitioner are stimulated in their thinking through the process so that aspects of practice are examined with depth and clarity. In other words, the conduct and process of the mentoring function are as important as the product and there is a strong emphasis on collaboration.

Stephens (1996) notes that there is a strong ethical element to mentoring which can involve helping practitioners to deal with such complex issues as children's rights, inclusion, diversity and social justice – all of which are important elements of informed early years practice. Mentors will therefore need, in addition to the personal qualities already noted, a commitment to open access to training, training as a co-operative venture, an enthusiasm for the practicalities of training and an understanding of mentoring as a means by which meanings about practice can be shared. This places mentoring at the heart of the reflective practice cycle. The mentor offers the practitioner both organisational and personal strategies for handling the challenges, responsibilities, pressures and stresses of early years practice – issues that are further developed in Chapter 3.

Being a mentor

Mentoring in the early years is a dynamic system of advice and support in the context of ongoing professional training and development which makes sense of reflective practice. The mentor helps this process by:

- Assisting the transmission of knowledge and skills.
- Guiding the induction and nurturing of practitioners.
- Linking theoretical models and philosophical approaches to practice.
- Reflecting standards and understanding of quality issues.
- Promoting shared good practice and professional values.

- Presenting solutions to professional challenges.
- Enabling the exercise of professional judgement.
- Focusing on the ability and potential of the practitioner.
- Enhancing the development of individuals and organisations.
- Drawing on and developing the research base for the sector.

> **PAUSE FOR THOUGHT**
>
> What will be the criteria and prerequisites for success as a mentor? How can the mentor ensure that both parties involved in the relationship have the same understanding of the role?

It may be helpful here to acknowledge that there are different models of mentoring. Clutterbuck (2004) describes a distinction between mentoring which is essentially 'developmental' or 'sponsoring' in its purpose. The difference being that the sponsoring model reflects situations where power and control in the relationship are not shared – the mentor has the primary responsibility for managing the process. As a result strategies and styles utilised by the mentor will be more directive, such as coaching or guiding. (This is outlined later in the chapter.) Non-directive styles such as counselling and facilitating are more suited to the developmental model, which is concerned with personal and professional change through reflection on experiences.

Whilst this may be an oversimplified interpretation of the two models, the point is that the developmental model is more suited to the early years context because of the value base and traditions noted above. The development model is a balance of formal and informal arrangements, where formal interventions enable planning and will give meaning to the mentoring process. The fact that this also supports the practitioner in their responses to experience enables the relationship to flourish through more informal interventions. This should not detract from the importance of being clear about contexts, boundaries and outcomes, as discussed in the context of good practice below.

In short, the early years mentor will operate within an appropriately staged framework of facilitating the development of the practitioner. This developmental framework will take account of needs but also operate on the basis of professional expectations to which all partners to the training of the practitioner agree. The discussion, negotiation and agreement of the mentoring framework are described by Wilkin (1992) as prerequisite for good practice.

Common themes for good practice: managing the process, ethics, training

The general principles noted above stress the importance of clarity in defining the mentor role. This clarity must also be extended to include a clear 'contract' between mentor and practitioner. As stated, the precise nature of the contract will reflect the context and purpose of the mentoring – for example, the practice mentor in work-based foundation degrees will be facilitating the outcomes of the programme in the first instance, rather than the agenda set by the workplace organisation. A visiting mentor teacher will be promoting national quality frameworks and local interpretation of standards for practice and may be involved in 'coaching' related skills to a group rather than an individual – whatever the context an early agreement and understanding about roles, responsibilities and expectations of the members of the partnership is crucial to any criteria for 'success'. Confidentiality is paramount to professionalism and is an underpinning requirement for successful mentoring in that it promotes trusting relationships – a prerequisite for honest, constructive evaluation and self-assessment in supported reflective practice.

In drawing up the mentoring contract, examples of best practice in all guidance emphasise the need for a discussion and agreement on what is expected within the relationship

Expectations of the mentor	*Expectations on the practitioner*
S/he is professionally competent, has a current knowledge base, responds to needs, manages the process, gives time in preparation, observation and feedback, keeps confidentiality, believes in the potential of the practitioner.	S/he is realistic in expectations of the mentor, accepts their own responsibilities for the process, is willing to action plan or set the direction for self-assessment, is willing to be challenged, behaves appropriately towards 'third parties' (e.g. the course tutor/leader and/or work-based line manager, whatever is appropriate to the context), keeps confidentiality.

PAUSE FOR THOUGHT

Why is discussion and agreement necessary at the start of a mentoring contract? What pitfalls might it help to avoid? What would be the role of the 'manager' in facilitating this agreement?

It may be useful to explore these issues by thinking about the ideal 'product'. All good mentoring contracts/relationships described in terms of the developmental model are reciprocal, based on trust and mutual respect, and will come to an end which is usually negotiated in advance. The relationship and process will be characterised by a high degree of mutual learning – indeed, a prime benefit for the mentor is the intellectual challenge that opportunities for a 'reflective space' will provide for self-development, continuing contact with practice networks and enhanced management skills. The practitioner will feel able to begin winding down the contact as s/he is able to identify positive outcomes and celebrate 'success' (however defined) within the process. The practitioner will move to new sources of learning and opportunities for reflective practice as s/he is able to identify strategies for working through challenges and choices independently. A good 'mentee' may go on to become an effective mentor and continue the cascade of reflective practice with other colleagues. Contact may continue informally if the mentoring was workplace-based rather than externally driven. Overall, the establishment of clear goals and expectations in the contracting stage avoids conflict. Time given at the beginning of the process to thinking about the conduct of the relationship and its end will hopefully avoid the difficulties presented when, for example, a practitioner might be overly dependent on the mentor, or confidentiality principles are not clearly understood.

The 'manager' of the mentor programme therefore has an interest in allowing time for the contracting process. Good practice also suggests a management commitment to mentoring *per se* to the extent that there will be support systems in place such as mentor training, reward and release for the full range of mentor activities. Dedicated mentor group meetings could be useful in enabling mentors to establish their own support networks. Thought will have been given to an ethical code of practice and clarity of roles between the mentor and the line manager, as noted above. In the training context, the manager will facilitate appropriate participation of the mentor in the planning and organisation of the student/practitioner's training in order to enhance the credibility and effectiveness of the mentor role. Again, the contribution of mentoring to overall quality of organisations cannot be ignored and is increasingly incorporated into management training for early years practitioners at all levels of continuing professional development. It should also be stated that the manager's role will be to ensure the effectiveness of the mentor by encouraging the support and co-operation of all colleagues relevant to the process.

Management of good practice is challenging. It is as well to acknowledge that the early years model of mentoring may involve practitioner contact with 'multiple mentors'. As a specific example, Smith and West-Burnham (1993) identify that there may be five possible practitioner contacts with a greater or lesser degree of mentor responsibility for trainee teachers. Foundation degree students may encounter a similar number – module tutors, course academic tutors, professional critical friend, practice mentor – in work-based programmes. In a sector where resources are scarce it is necessary to be certain that there is a clear demarcation in roles and responsibilities in such cases, as cost implications for courses and employers alike may retain barriers to training that work-based programmes have struggled to break down. Those practitioners in contact with mentor teachers may also feel that the service duplicates advice and support roles taken by EYDCP officers or field workers within bodies such as the Pre-school Learning Alliance. Clarity is the essence, as noted above; a key difference in the later examples would be that these roles would involve group rather than individual mentoring so all partners to the mentoring process will need a clear understanding of the precise nature of their own activity and its contribution to mentoring in a wider context. Managing the implementation of a mentoring structure is examined more fully in Chapter 5. To conclude an understanding of what mentoring is and might involve in the early years, an introduction to the range of different mentoring behaviours will assist new mentors to identify activities that suit their own role and setting.

Mentoring: activities within the process

Early years mentors should be clear that they are operating in a specific context, with specific outcomes, with specific expectations and through a process based on a combination and variations of the activities (Pegg, 2000) shown in Table 1.1.

Table 1.1   Mentoring activities

Mentoring – the classic guide who will share their knowledge in a way that empowers others.	**Coaching** – a coach responds to short-term skill-based needs. The coach will encourage, equip and enable others to increase their skills.
Modelling – literally to model effective behaviours and attitudes, demonstrating successful strategies.	**Counselling** – acting as a reflective listener, the counsellor assists others to find their own solutions to problems by posing pertinent questions rather than by directing action.
Teaching – will inspire and enthuse, helping others to integrate knowledge into daily practice.	**Being a 'buddy'** – a system used by some organisations to help with settling in. Sometimes called Mentors but quite distinct from the full mentor role.
Advising – a source of specialist knowledge.	**Leading** – having drive and vision to engage others and deliver results.

PAUSE FOR THOUGHT

Which of the 'behaviours' defined in Table 1.1 most closely describe the activities of your own mentoring role? Can the activities be adapted for group mentoring as well as individuals? Are some activities mutually exclusive? Do others have the potential for overlap with other professionals involved in supporting the student practitioner?

Drawing on a repertoire of behaviours enables the mentor to respond sensitively to the changing needs of the practitioner as the relationship evolves. Some of these activities are more directive than others. The clarity of the mentoring contract is crucial to the understanding of both parties about the appropriateness of the mentor's responses. For example, a 'classical' mentor will usually avoid giving advice unless first acknowledging a specific change of role in order to do so. Alternatively, a teacher/guide may also coach or demonstrate specific skills but might not see it as part of this more directive role to counsel or propose alternative strategies for the student's practice. If roles and functions are not clear, this can lead to a great deal of frustration for the practitioner and jeopardise the relationship and its ultimate success. At issue is the operation of power and the extent to which it can be shared within certain of the roles or activities shown. The developmental model favours 'power sharing', so the effective mentor will respond to the need of the practitioner with consistent behaviours. Both partners should agree if the mentor has to 're-position' within the contract in order to facilitate different responses to specific situations. In the variety of possible mentoring activities and responses the nature and type of feedback will also be affected. It must be stressed that the underlying principle of transparency at all stages of the process and how it is communicated will constantly reflect on the outcomes for mentor and practitioner alike.

Where next?

> **PAUSE FOR THOUGHT**
>
> **Reflections for further self-development**
>
> Mentors may be more confident in some of the activities described in Table 1.1 than others. Do certain activities suit your own philosophy more than others? Which activities fit most closely with the developmental model of mentoring? Does the context of your own role mean that you are driven to use a different model of mentoring or be involved in activities that are at odds with your personal style and ideas?

These questions are intended to mirror some of the thoughts that motivate mentors in a reflective process to seek further professional development and training in order to resolve areas of tension and challenge within the role. In addition such questions will give the opportunity for focused reading within this publication and for the following chapter in particular. How individual mentors develop their practice will depend largely upon resolving the personal dimension of motivation for and within the role – facing their own challenges and responding to difficulties and tensions. Mentors need mentoring, and this facility must be found in the workplace, however it is defined, as well as through continuing training.

Points to remember

● Mentoring is a recognised activity concerned with the supported professional development of practitioners in
work-based practice.

● The nature of mentoring is determined by the 'culture' –
traditions and philosophy – of the organisation concerned.

● Early years mentoring is shaped by sector requirements
as well as specific institutions and settings.

● Effective practice for mentors in the early years can draw
on ethics and models of good practice established in other
situations, e.g. business and teacher training contexts.

● Mentors will share common characteristics and activities, whilst outcomes of the mentoring process will be
context-specific.

● Mentors will also reflect on their practice and will require a
supportive and supported framework in which to do so.

2

The mentor as 'the one in the middle'

Sue Callan and Eryl Copp

This chapter examines key issues raised in Chapter 1 from the point of view of the mentor in practice. It is not possible within the constraints of this book to unpick specific examples for each and every context, but by offering models drawn from our own experience we provide a series of strategies to enable mentors to get started and then to evaluate and reflect on challenges encountered in practice. As the chapter progresses, discussion points and pauses for thought give way to key points which bring together techniques for effective practice. The chapter outlines:

- How to establish confidentiality, credibility and clarity.
- How to recognise and adopt styles of mentor behaviour.
- How to work towards a model of collaborative practice.
- Critical influences on the mentor role.
- A basic template with which to assess experiences encountered in practice.

Terminology

It is necessary to define terms that are used in this chapter. The term 'student practitioner' is used instead of 'mentee', as it covers the widest possible spectrum of contexts. The mentor remains as role-specific but as a general term will also encompass other workplace relationships involving mentoring, for example the role of a 'professional critical friend'. For ease of use, the term 'senior practitioner' is used to cover those roles of supervisor, manager or teacher to be found in early years settings. The 'setting' will cover all possible provision and services within the sector. The 'mentor contract', as described in Chapter 1, is the negotiated agreement between the mentor and student practitioner which defines the purpose of the mentoring process, agrees conduct of meetings/observations and the scope of the mentor role, agrees the expectations of all parties and indicates a time scale for completion with review dates as necessary. Although the term 'contract' suggests a formal written agreement, there will be aspects of it that are discussed and interpreted according to individual requirements.

Key principles in establishing effective relationships

Mentoring has been described in Chapter 1 as a role that involves working with people from a range of backgrounds and, occasionally, across institutions – based on collaboration as a core strategy. In this role, the mentor must try to facilitate relationships within which it is possible to pose challenging personal and professional questions in order for the student practitioner to understand theory, practice and day-to-day experiences – in other words, promoting reflection in practice. This model of mentoring is based on key ethical principles of confidentiality, credibility and clarity, all of which engender trust between those involved. It is important to remember that the mentor may be visiting or working within the setting, and that the external mentor may have to strive harder to achieve the key ethical principles than the internal mentor who already has the advantage of familiarity.

Confidentiality

Mentoring will invariably take place within an ethical framework of good practice where *confidentiality* is paramount. It is also one of the most complex areas in terms of the fine line that the mentor treads in maintaining the contract made with the student practitioner within the setting and adherence to their own professional mandate. In order to avoid ambiguity and misunderstanding ground rules for confidentiality must be owned by all parties, explicit from the outset and renegotiated if necessary. Mentors must also be prepared to acknowledge their own thoughts and attitudes towards confidentiality and be certain, especially if they are visiting/external mentors, that they can identify the point at which confidentiality is superseded by the need to share information with others as discussed below.

Credibility

As a professional principle, confidentiality also enhances and supports the *credibility* of the mentor. Credibility is essential to the ability to mediate between various parties involved in the mentoring contract. The mentor must strive to establish credibility with everyone involved in the process in order to effectively support learning and reflective practice. It is worth considering whether the same kinds of qualities that establish credibility with the student practitioner will earn the respect of the senior practitioner. For example, the mentor often models creativity for the student when applying theory to experience or presenting alternative approaches and ideas; this quality may not be as welcomed by a senior practitioner, particularly if s/he feels that established practice within their setting is being questioned or challenged. A mentor must be able to draw upon their own integrity coupled with strategies that ensure suggestions are well received, and where appropriate make use of alternative methods such as 'reverse mentoring', which is discussed later in this chapter.

PAUSE FOR THOUGHT AND DISCUSSION POINTS

Every registered provision will have clear policies and procedures in place for the sharing of information and concerns. The challenge for the external mentor as 'the one in the middle' will be when the concern is about the person or persons in charge and the mentor must refer to Ofsted or the Local Authority. Anyone who undertakes the role of mentor must understand the process and be prepared to act accordingly should the need arise.

Consider the legislative requirements for confidentiality within a range of early years settings.

1 How can the mentor be confident that they would feel empowered to report 'issues' such as a breach in registration requirements or a child protection concern?

2 If bad practice is observed how will this be shared with the appropriate person or organisation?

The qualities that the mentor demonstrates to establish credibility with the senior practitioner would be those that emphasise professionalism, weighted by experience, qualifications and success as a practitioner. This is seen as a priority strategy for those getting started in the mentor role, as it will assist with establishing and maintaining the contract within the setting. In order to achieve and maintain credibility the mentor must pay heed to:

- The perceptions of the student practitioner, senior practitioners and others as to the role and professional status of the mentor.
- Effective strategies for engaging with the student practitioner.
- The need for credibility to be established as an important aspect of the mentor's role in supporting, offering advice and sharing knowledge.

With credibility a mentor can become a role model, a counsellor and befriender whilst remembering that sometimes an experienced senior practitioner with credibility is better placed to provide focused feedback.

> ### PAUSE FOR THOUGHT FOR MENTORS
>
> On reflection do you have the necessary qualities that give you credibility as a mentor? If you are unsure, you might consider using the following questions in order to analyse and evaluate this.
>
> 1 How do you ensure your professional qualifications and experiences are known by the student practitioner and others in the organisation?
>
> 2 How do the qualifications and experiences you bring to the mentoring role match the needs of the student practitioner?
>
> 3 Can you find a way of assessing your own professional credibility with your peers, in order to increase the likelihood of earning respect from others?

Clarity of role

Having considered credibility, the importance of *clarity of role* is also identified as an essential component of a contract and relates closely to both confidentiality and credibility. The mentors should negotiate aspects of the contract with senior practitioners in order to achieve clarity of role. For visiting mentors, who are not only 'in the middle' of workplace relationships but may also be outsiders, this presents a particular challenge – senior practitioners need to be a part of the process if the student practitioner is to derive maximum benefit. The mentor is therefore 'in the middle', whether or not s/he is working as part of the internal organisational relationships or representing a set of external requirements.

To be effective, an internal mentor needs to be clear about their role in relation to the management structure of the setting. Perhaps the role is a personal relationship with the student practitioner, possibly as a 'buddy' or a 'professional critical friend' to a less experienced or new colleague. Alternatively, the mentor may be someone who is required to participate in appraisal of the student practitioner in a more formalised role concerned with the management of the setting and training requirements. Once again, if the mentor has due regard to the key principles already discussed, together with a clear understanding of the purpose of the role and its boundaries, this will underpin the success of the mentor in challenging and nurturing the student practitioner.

Mentor behaviour for different situations

It is helpful to remember that a mentor (either internal or external) also has a range of *behaviours* to draw on. These are described in Chapter 1 in terms of behaviour that will either enhance the development of the student practitioner or is more directive in terms of the needs of the setting. Hamilton (1993) identifies three behaviours when the mentor may be acting as a:

- **Coach:** as a directive means of support, offering instruction or demonstration when needed and setting goals.
- **Counsellor:** encouraging and supporting, giving clarity and discussing options.
- **Role model:** a source of information and a standard by which the student practitioner can evaluate their own performance.

These behaviours when applied to the mentoring role will inevitably overlap and will help set the tone for different interactions with the student practitioner, as well as influencing the overall style of mentoring in terms of the more directive approach which involves coaching or guiding and the non-directive or developmental approach of counselling and sharing of information. The effective mentor will be prepared to adopt all the behaviours at different points in the relationship. Some of these behaviours will emerge as a result of the purpose of the mentoring role (as defined by the contract), and, for the same reason, others may not be helpful because of the particular context. Mentors may also feel that particular behaviour in the role is intuitive – such as counselling, reflection or relationship functions – but it should be remembered that in modelling such behaviours the mentor is assisting the other parties in the contract to identify positive interactions for the workplace.

Developing positive interactions

The pitfalls of being 'the one in the middle' can be avoided by recognising which behaviour suits particular situations. Whatever the context – mentoring as part of an internal, democratic management structure supporting professional development, or as an external representative of qualification or quality accreditation frameworks – the mentor must work hard to establish positive contact with both the student and the senior practitioner. This will be facilitated by the behaviours noted, but will also be enhanced if senior practitioners recognise the value of mentoring and have a commitment to it. There are benefits for all partners involved when this is established, either in the ethos of the setting or negotiation by the mentor. For example, Clutterbuck (2004) suggests a practical advantage to the senior practitioner when some 'reverse mentoring' takes place, as mentioned previously. These are situations where the mentor's work with the student will involve senior practitioners in a way that will keep managers in touch with current or emerging practice and provide positive ways of evaluating and developing their own management skills. In these situations the student will have in-house support and encouragement that will maintain the motivation to learn. In particular, the student practitioner will experience best practice in terms of professional behaviours in the workplace. The mentor will also have the confidence that there will be a supportive framework for dealing with feedback in the workplace.

PAUSE FOR THOUGHT

An example of 'reverse mentoring'

A student practitioner who is an employee in a school is being 'too confident' and making personal decisions without consulting others. This is causing some problems within the team and with parents. The senior practitioner is the class teacher, who is finding difficulty in dealing with the situation.

1 How might the mentor support the senior practitioner in helping the student to understand an appropriate way to deal with the professional hierarchy without undermining confidence?

2 Identify ways in which the senior practitioner skills are enhanced through this experience.

A model for excellent practice

The above example demonstrates that both mentor and senior practitioner have an interest in helping the development of the student practitioner. The mentor who is able to build on this shared interest will involve the senior practitioner in the most positive way possible. The workplace functions of the senior practitioner role can be integrated in, and are recognised as complementary to, the mentoring process. For example, in the management of the workplace; the senior practitioner engages in aspects of directive behaviour which involve performance appraisal, goal and target setting and the identification of opportunities for further challenge based on the needs of the setting. This has a close relationship with the developmental behaviour of the mentor towards the student practitioner. The combination of the two roles – directive and developmental – mean that the student is able to consider goals in both personal and professional contexts. Clutterbuck (2004) outlines this partnership as an ideal model for mentor practice; in effect, the mentor who is able to develop and work within this collaborative model will be highly effective in negotiating the key issues identified earlier – confidentiality, credibility and clarity – and well placed to deal appropriately with the challenges posed by being in the middle of a web of complex personal and professional interactions. The second part of this chapter provides an overview of some of the challenges facing the mentor and outlines strategies that enable a positive response and outcome.

Meanwhile ... in the real world

Anything that affects the positive esteem and self-concept of the student practitioner is a challenge to the work of the mentor because of the impact on independent learning and reflective processes. The student practitioner is faced with a complex interaction of elements that can enhance or impede professional development. In fact, all parties to the mentoring process may be subject to influences that can have considerable impact on the quality of personal and professional relationships in settings. This part of the chapter examines some of these influences and identifies ways in which mentors can begin to identify and deal with the impact on the mentoring role. The aim is to offer a 'template' with which to assess challenging situations – an approach that will enable the mentor to 'depersonalise' areas of conflict or difficulty, and consider, for each challenge, *'What exactly is the problem here?'* The strategy of mentoring as a 'professional friend' is also explored in relation to some of the positive characteristics of the early years work-force.

KEY POINTS

Critical issues influencing mentor practice

- *Workforce developments and policy*: at national, local and setting level – specifically qualification and training requirements.

- *Workplace culture, relationships*: hierarchies, ethos, morale and team dynamics.

- *Gender balance of the work force*: the influence on mentoring style.

- *Personal issues*: the self-concept of the student practitioner and feedback that promotes reflective practice.

- *The senior practitioner*: attitudes and action.

- *Your own confidence* and performance in the role.

- *Motivation* of the mentor and student practitioner.

The mentor in the midst of such influences will utilise various approaches when negotiating a way forward – whether adopting the directive or the developmental approaches already discussed. Although judgements will be made in good faith, care and sensitivity are needed when considering an appropriate response to a challenging situation.

Qualification and training are an issue that impacts on the role of the mentor because of its effect on student practitioner self-esteem and confidence. Government models of excellence in practice supported by research increasingly reflect the traditions, philosophy and theoretical foundations claimed by the early years sector. The mentor is 'in the middle' because s/he may well be representing such models, as well as having to challenge the ideas and practice of student practitioners whose motivation to learn may in itself be challenged by the material conditions of the workplace. Such students are not always open to reflection on their values and attitudes, using their 'real world' daily experience like a security blanket in order to resist changing ideas about practice in the sector – hence the subtitle of this section.

KEY POINTS

Qualifications

- The government is committed to making the early years work force a world-class, highly skilled and valued profession.

- There is renewed emphasis on training with many qualifications available.

- It is recognised as good practice in early years to be ready to reflect upon, challenge and extend learning.

- A mentor may need to be prepared to advise on qualifications available locally.

- Part of the mentor role is to encourage professional development– this may be challenging, particularly with long-serving and experienced practitioners who have not considered or may see little benefit in undertaking academic study.

- Good teamwork is enhanced by shared respect for the qualifications and experiences of colleagues.

- The Effective Provision of Pre-school Education project (DfES, 2002) emphasises that outcomes for early years are enhanced when practitioners are well qualified both practically and academically.

The self-concept and -esteem of practitioners in the early years sector can be influenced by the hierarchy within individual workplaces; rigid hierarchies could be detrimental to the integrated working relationships and combined service provision promoted in emerging national policy. In day-to-day practice rigid hierarchies can also be a threat to the success and effectiveness of the mentor because they do not always create an enabling environment for professional development.

Negative dynamics within teams may be evident through high staff turnover and low morale. The mentor will need some means of becoming quickly aware of team dynamics in individual settings of which the student practitioner is a part.

Formal workforce surveys support the accepted view that early years work teams are usually predominantly female. This will have an impact on the nature and quality of adult interactions in settings. Whilst it is impossible to do justice to the complexity of *gender influence* here, mentors in the sector can consider some general points. Vance (1979) acknowledges that the relationships of women in the workplace are usually characterised by friendship and mutual support as they negotiate the working environment. This can be both a strength and a challenge in practice, depending on the dynamics of individual workplaces, but early years mentors can adopt this approach when considering ways of supporting the student practitioner.

The mentor supporting both practitioner and nursery manager

How to mentor as a 'professional friend'

Inexperienced mentors should be aware that there is inevitably a blurring of personal and professional roles when mentoring as a 'professional friend'. This more personally based relationship can affect the clarity of contract previously examined in terms of establishing professional boundaries. However, it is the 'friendship' element that enables the student practitioner to gain empowerment. Positive feelings and responses can be generated by the close relationship that exists. Gardiner (2003) points out that, whilst formal mentoring cannot replace the informal systems that are part of everyday work relationships, mentors and student practitioners will benefit if a 'professional friendship' can be established within the contract because this promotes the self-esteem of the student. Whilst aspiring to this type of style, mentors should be wary of pitfalls. Initially very nurturing, there is a danger that the closeness of the friendship can have an adverse effect as the student practitioner develops as a professional – relating to issues of separation and termination of the contract as discussed in Chapter 1.

The familiarity of the role of professional friend brings its own challenges. It is therefore important that clear boundaries are agreed from the outset. The depth of trust and mutual respect on which the 'friendship' is established can be compromised if one of the parties loses confidence in the other. The mentor as professional friend must be prepared to manage the situation and not let over-familiarity undermine the relationship. The influence of a senior practitioner within the setting may be used to mediate in order to bring the relationship back on track or to facilitate renegotiation of the contract.

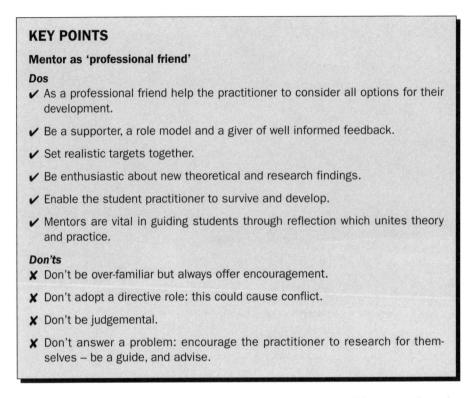

Within any mentoring contract the student practitioner will bring to the relationship personal issues acquired through life experiences. Similarly, s/he will contribute these influences to the *team and group dynamic* within the workplace, interacting and reacting with others and their responses to him/her. Just as early years practitioners need to develop positive relationships with young children to promote development and learning, so the student practitioner needs to feel liked and to have a sense of 'belonging' in the mentoring process. For the mentor, this raises the challenge of giving feedback which takes account of all these personal features but which will enable the student practitioner to stand back from the personal dimension of the job role and reflect back on it. The mentor will challenge ideas about practice whilst nurturing and developing the individual and helping the student practitioner to see things that they have long ceased to notice about themselves. These issues are further explored in Chapter 3.

One of the main roles of the mentor is to motivate a student practitioner within a team. The mentor must treat the team with respect and empathy in order to ensure the best outcomes for the student practitioner and, indirectly, the children. Team issues have already been identified as influential to the mentor and the senior practitioner is a key player. This person may be both senior *and* a student practitioner, trying to reflect on and adapt practice in a way that maintains cohesion in the setting. S/he may not be a student but balancing a number of conflicting priorities as a manager and therefore a great deal of sensitivity is needed by the mentor in involving the senior practitioner as a partner. However the senior practitioner perceives the situation, it must also be acknowledged that s/he is subject to the same influences outlined above. The crucial difference is that the way s/he perceives the leadership role, which is undoubtedly challenging, will determine the quality of experience of mentoring for the whole workplace. One of the mentor's most important functions is to develop a shared vision among staff. This is clearly evident in the case study in Chapter 6. A key strategy for all mentors will therefore be to establish a positive relationship with the senior practitioner, building on the initial techniques outlined at the beginning of this chapter.

The senior practitioner's attitude to training and professional development will fundamentally influence the effectiveness of the mentor for the student practitioner in the workplace. The attitude towards mentoring in particular can result in either a supportive and nurturing environment – or a situation where the mentor has to draw on all available resources in developing this important

PAUSE FOR THOUGHT

In the following examples the senior practitioner will be required to give substantial practical and study support to portfolio building as part of assessment. Contrast the responses given to the student practitioner's request to attend courses.

- A senior practitioner asked 'what was in it' for her, Why should she agree to time off work for her employee, increase her salary and ultimately lose a good member of staff as other/better employment opportunities arose in the future? She appeared not to see the relevance of the particular qualification and declined to be involved in 'more work'.

- A day nursery was unable to send a representative to a pre-course information event, so a visit was arranged. After hearing the details the senior practitioner was enthusiastic to be involved in the whole 'training thing'.

1 Why might these responses differ?

2 What are the implications for the mentor?

3 What are the implications for the student practitioner?

relationship.

These scenarios giving pause for thought are based on actual experiences encountered by mentors in practice. The emotional and physical energy required to deal with such tensions, particularly where a senior practitioner is negative, can be considerable for the mentor and the student practitioner alike. However, the fears articulated by the first employer are very real for those responsible for settings in a sector that is short of staff in key parts of the work force. Even where the initial response is positive it is common for mentors to have to work hard to keep senior practitioners involved as requirements for continuing reflection and evaluation extend to all aspects of practice – for example, with regard to the framework of outcomes for *Every Child Matters* (DfES, 2003).

Being a mentor: bringing it all together

> ### CASE STUDY
>
> **Dealing with critical influences in practice**
>
> A student practitioner has a new role in the setting. S/he has supervisory responsibilities reflecting senior practitioner requirements. At present s/he is endeavouring to get to know the children whilst not feeling supported by the staff team. S/he has told her mentor that she has no evidence of planning and is clearly struggling. S/he has started to resist feedback from the mentor and has cancelled a couple of meetings at short notice.
>
> 1 Which critical influences are at play here?
>
> 2 What do you do?
>
> 3 How can you involve the senior practitioner and the whole team?

Zachary (2000) suggests that this is where the mentor must encourage the student practitioner to move forward to embrace new challenges. The mentor should be ready to provide feedback and ask challenging questions. This is truly an opportunity for reflection-in-action, a concept that is explored in Chapter 3. It will be helpful to encourage the student practitioner to develop a step-by-step action plan, and to ask for feedback on that plan from all those involved in his/her professional development. To be effective, this strategy requires the support of the senior practitioner, who will have knowledge of the day-to-day routines of the workplace and the wider dynamics involved. If a supportive relationship with the senior practitioner has already been established a shared discussion may help revive the declining self-confidence of the student practitioner. If other critical influences are involved, such as professional jealousies in the team, each will need to be addressed as part of the review process.

For all challenging situations an effective approach by the mentor would be to consider carefully the impact of any critical influences on the progress of the student, and plan a response that draws on the repertoire of mentoring strategies in order to maintain the clarity of action necessary. The role of the mentor is *not* to solve problems for the student practitioner but to provide a framework of approaches within which to facilitate self-management.

Once the mentor has considered and identified which critical influences are contributing to difficult situations experienced in the mentoring process, the following key points for 'troubleshooting ' can be used to identify ways of moving forward. This is supported by Parsloe and Wray (2000) and enables mentors to intervene appropriately to address complex situations. The process involved is cyclical and should ideally include the senior practitioner in order to consolidate the collaborative approach described in the earlier part of the chapter.

> **KEY POINTS**
>
> **Troubleshooting**
>
> - *Keep in mind the purpose of the mentoring relationship*. Review the contract and any personal professional development plan.
>
> - *Review goals*. They will no doubt change as the student practitioner begins to develop professionally.
>
> - *Encourage self-management*. Adjust the balance of power to enable the relationship to continue as appropriate.
>
> - *Support through feedback which builds on success*. Confidence maintains motivation.
>
> - *Assist in evaluation*. It may be appropriate to amend the contract.

In all cases the aim is to maintain the professional relationship through an evolving contract. Any review may raise personal issues for the student practitioner therefore s/he needs to continue to feel supported within clear boundaries.

Mentors also need supported opportunities to reflect on their skills and qualities in order to develop in this challenging and stimulating role. The use of a 'SWOT' checklist may assist both the student practitioner and the mentor:

- *Strengths*. Make a list of the strengths that enable you to carry out your role professionally.
- *Weaknesses*. What areas need further development?
- *Opportunities*. What opportunities would you look forward to taking?
- *Threats*. What sort of pitfalls might you experience?

For mentors involved with student practitioners on training courses it is important to have an awareness of any programme aims, assessment and content. The mentor is not always part of the delivery team and must therefore be confident in the aspects of any programme as part of their role in supporting student practitioners.

Mentors may also be asked to take a role in the assessment of course work, which in itself presents other issues, since the requirement to be involved in assessment may bring extra pressure to the role. Whilst mentors are not usually asked to take responsibility for 'pass' or 'fail' decisions, they may be involved in moderation of grades awarded. If their student practitioners are experiencing difficulty an added burden is placed on the mentor, who might become concerned about their own competence in the role if students fail.

Here the self-concept of the mentor is shown to be subject to the same forces as that of the student practitioner and, as such, the personal and professional credibility of the mentor discussed, as part of 'first principles', is potentially undermined. Thoughtful management of schemes, including support for mentors, as discussed in Chapter 5, can alleviate some of these issues.

Parsloe and Wray (2000) encourage mentors to bear in mind that student practitioners usually view them as 'job coaches', so that it is unrealistic to assume that there will be no form of 'assessment' involved in the mentoring contract. The core principle is that the quality of the relationship is at the heart of effective mentoring and that this will be the means by which mentor and student practitioner together overcome any challenges presented. The motivation, attitude and support of the mentor have a greater correlation with the effectiveness of the process than other factors such as mentor skills.

Points to remember

Throughout this chapter principles guiding practice are extended to incorporate a number of straightforward techniques to help the mentor to maintain professionalism and credibility as a facilitator of learning through reflective practice. It is proposed that the 'ideal' model is 'collaborative mentoring' and that this will require commitment to teamwork principles. All mentors are encouraged to remember:

- That good team work requires all individuals to recognise and value others.
- To establish and maintain communication with other colleagues.
- To be positively assertive and confident in themselves in order to instil confidence in others.
- To always demonstrate good practice and professionalism.

The important message is that the mentor is genuinely 'in the middle', not simply between the student and senior practitioner but in among a range of critical interrelated personal and professional issues which together influence relationships in settings. The mentor ultimately draws the whole thing together and holds the key to a successful experience for everyone involved.

📖 Further reading

Hamilton, R. (1993) *Mentoring*. London: The Industrial Society. This book describes the competences and strengths of an effective mentor and identifies some of the approaches a mentor may adopt.

3

Being reflective
Encouraging and teaching reflective practice
Kate Fowler and Alison Robins

This chapter begins by considering what we mean by reflective practice and whether or not it is instinctive or intuitive. Further thought is given to mentors themselves as reflective practitioners and the ways in which reflective practice can be modelled and taught. Later, reflective practice is viewed through a case study that demonstrates how an action–reflection cycle leads to personal professional development and potentially, improvements within the workplace. The concluding discussion emphasises the important role reflective practice plays in improving quality within early years settings, ourselves and those we mentor as practitioners and lifelong learners.

Reflective thinking and reflective practice

Socrates (399 BC) attached great importance to critical thinking because of the real contribution he thought it made to our everyday lives. In recent years much has been written about 'critical thinking' or 'reflective practice'. Dewey (1933: 9), when talking about 'reflective thinking', defined it as the 'active, persistent and careful consideration of any belief or supposed form of knowledge …'. It is this 'reflective thinking' that enables all practitioners to develop personally and professionally, as it ensures that issues meaningful and relevant within the context of their own practice (everyday life) can be considered, lessons learnt and changes (progress) made. Much of the most effective learning happens to us in real life with real situations and real people. This thought is in line with what Dewey said about learning being 'a process of discovery' (in Handy, 1993: 45) but we have to be willing to actually engage in reflection, self-appraisal and development. Another significant writer in the area of reflective practice is Schön (cited in Pollard and Tann, 1994), who suggests that as practitioners we can either 'reflect–in-action', which is reflection taking place during an event or experience, or 'reflect-on-action', which is reflecting after the event.

CASE STUDY

Context
Baby room in a nursery.

The experience
Jo, as an experienced nursery nurse, cares for seven-month-old Poppy in a local nursery. Highly determined and extremely inquisitive, Poppy sits strongly and reaches determinedly for objects all around her. Together on the play rug Jo observes that Poppy is particularly interested in the tower cups. She notices that Poppy constantly homes in on the cups and notes that she can find, pick up, hold, suck, blow, bang and drop and retrieve them! Jo starts to build a tower with the cups, ensuring that Poppy still has command of the playthings and that she is close enough to reach the tower. Excited, flailing hands dislodge the tower – CRASH! Jo rebuilds. Poppy crashes! Wild laughter. A great game of 'build and crash' develops. Jo builds, Poppy crashes!

Reflection on the experience
It can be seen that, having noted what Poppy was able to do, Jo, *reflected-in-action* and, by structuring a new activity, attempted to move Poppy's learning and development forward. With Jo facilitating, a great deal of learning did take place, not least that Poppy had an early introduction into cause and effect!

Later in the day, as part of normal practice, Jo evaluated the time spent with Poppy. Jo decided that during their next play session she would introduce new building materials to include different textures and a variety of sizes with a view to further developing Poppy's skills.

By reviewing the outcomes of their shared experience Jo *reflected-on-action*, allowing her to consider a 'next step' for Poppy and plan more activities and new experiences.

All the signs indicate that Jo also recognises the benefit of these types of reflection on her personal learning and her professional development.

PAUSE FOR THOUGHT

The purpose of both 'reflection in action' and 'reflection on action' is to improve future action and therefore practice.

Fowler and Russel (1998) looked at student teachers' use of profiles to support their learning, and found that most learners considered 'learning through reflection on practice' as extremely important to their development. There were, however, some learners who seemed to have a very real misconception of and sometimes a dismissive attitude towards the value of reflection for both their personal values and professional practice. Undertaking reflection on practice for these particular learners, who were also actively involved in children's learning and development, must surely be seen as crucial to their proficiency as practitioners and fundamental to their continued learning, particularly in the workplace. As mentors supporting practitioners we ourselves need to have an understanding of the importance of reflecting on our thoughts, values and practice and also have the ability to support practitioners in their understanding of the importance of this concept.

As workers in the field of early years, tutor/mentors of early years students/practitioners, and researchers into good practice and student development in early years courses, we fully endorse the notion of teaching and learning through critical reflective practice and personal and professional development which we should strive to model ourselves.

The following pause for thought indicates the importance of the development of reflective practice and consequently a reflective practitioner in the field of early years.

PAUSE FOR THOUGHT

Reflective practice

- Implies that practitioners are actively concerned about the aims and consequences of the work they are doing.
- Enables practitioners to monitor, evaluate and revise their own practice continuously.
- Requires an ability to look carefully at practice in order to support the development of new skills and understanding.
- Requires an open-minded attitude.
- Enhances professional learning and personal fulfilment through collaboration and dialogue between practitioners.

Is reflective practice instinctive or intuitive?

Before we consider how we can support our practitioners in their reflective practice it is worth considering if reflective action is dependent on learning how to reflect or if it is instinctive or intuitive? Referring again to Dewey, it is by his suggestion that we know intuitively that we need to do things in order to learn from our experiences and to deal with our expectations. More recently Atkinson and Claxton (2000) have pursued the notion of 'ways of thinking', 'learning' and how these are influenced by intuition. Their book is suggested as further reading at the end of this chapter.

While working with learners within a variety of courses it has become clear to us that there are some people who can intuitively see potential for personal and professional development in any situation. They are able to assess a situation and its worth, reflect upon and change things to ensure personal progress and maintain a favourable atmosphere in which their learning continues to take place. These changes or choices made during the course of their practice are largely intuitive because they see the need for action as being immediate.

CASE STUDY

Context
Year 2 art lesson. Twenty-nine children. Activity: mixing colours and decorating plant pots.

Intuitive action
It became very clear to the teacher within five minutes of beginning the activity that things were going to go disastrously owing to the layout of the activity and distribution of resources. She could see that the children could not access the materials they needed comfortably and the plant pots themselves were in one corner of the room rather than being spread out among the activity tables. She could see arguments arising about sharing of colours and a scramble for the pots once the paints had been mixed.

Whilst feeling rather 'hot under the collar' she reflected upon the situation and made the decision to abandon the lesson and clear away the paints and pots.

The children were initially disappointed but the practitioner discussed her decision and concerns with them and together they planned a way forward for the session for the following day. The children themselves came up with table layouts, material distribution and ideas for sharing when necessary. The lesson was a complete success.

Question
Would the same intuitive response be made by all practitioners?

Sometimes we as professionals working with small children in dynamic situations have little time to reach decisions, to even begin to ask questions such as 'How do I go on from here?' 'What do I do?' The 'heat of the moment' situations often need immediate and intuitive action. This links with Schön's 'reflection in action', and the ability to recognise when something has 'gone wrong' or 'not as planned' in practice helps with the development of a stronger, more confident practitioner.

But is this intuitive ability innate or learnt? Is it a personal characteristic that we are blessed with, or is this intuitive wisdom something, like theory and practice, that can be learnt and developed? It could be suggested that there are some people who strive to develop an existing and innate quality of intuitive wisdom and that it is a characteristic which is endemic in varying degrees in all of us. It's just waiting to be teased out during the process of learning and development. However, is this intuitive wisdom a necessary element to being a reflective early

Reflecting together on events from the day

years practitioner? If so, can an early years tutor/mentor teach a student/practitioner to be intuitive? We would say that the ability to act intuitively is there, in varying degrees, in all students/practitioners and it is the role of tutors/mentors engaged in the support, mentoring and teaching of these practitioners to further develop this innate intuition and thereby facilitate reflectiveness.

> **PAUSE FOR THOUGHT FOR MENTORS**
>
> Consider a moment of 'reflection in action' during your own practice. Consider how you might use your example to facilitate a practitioner's learning in terms of developing confidence in trusting their intuition and judgement.

Mentors as reflective practitioners

It could be argued that as mentors we should, first and foremost, challenge our own reflective skills. Are we truly reflective in our own practice? Have we learnt how to reflect, and if so how do we do it? Who supports us in this process? It is important to consider these questions from a very personal perspective before going on to consider how we encourage and teach those whom we are mentoring to reflect.

To take a very basic definition, it could be suggested that we consider reflective practice as simply 'thinking about what we have done, are doing or are going to do'. This makes it sound like an easy activity and for some people it may be more intuitive, as suggested above. However, for the vast majority of us, embarking upon the reflective process can be quite difficult.

PAUSE FOR THOUGHT

Note down a recent experience that has remained 'on your mind' since it happened. Have you reflected on this experience at all? Have you discussed the 'event' with anyone else? Has bringing this to mind now and writing it down moved you forward in your thoughts?

To reflect upon our work, our values or our actions really challenges our thinking, and if we find ourselves in a situation where we believe our thoughts have no importance we may well be reluctant to reflect on and share the outcomes. Potter and Richardson (1999: 34) outline such a situation where a discussion had been facilitated in order to encourage a reflective dialogue between a classroom team. 'The response was a long silence as the staff thought that their responses were not important or interesting enough to share with the group.' Interestingly, in 1995, a project called Principles into Practice (PiP; Blenkin and Kelly, 1997) found that in some of the most successful settings the less confident practitioners had to be encouraged and supported in reflecting upon their practice. To put the project into context, it focused on the quality of early years provision in England and considered that underpinning quality provision were the skills and expertise of early years practitioners. It found that the provision of quality within settings was related to the willingness of practitioners to be open to challenge and take ownership of their practice (Blenkin and Kelly, 1997).

This openness sounds easy but, from personal experience, we have heard teaching assistants make comments such as 'Why should I say what I think? I'm only a teaching assistant.' Similar situations may be faced and need handling by us as mentors. We may have had experiences of our voices and thoughts not being valued and heard but we should consider that we may also be supporting practitioners who find themselves in this position. The challenge is then for us to reflect upon how such situations might be handled sensitively for all involved, an area that is explored in Chapter 2.

PAUSE FOR THOUGHT FOR MENTORS

How might I respond to a practitioner who says that her line manager/colleague is not interested in what she has to say?

Reflective practice is easily encouraged and facilitated by simply asking questions. Within the context of this chapter and the practitioners with whom you will be working these questions will focus mainly on improving and maintaining standards (of provision and self). The first step, as a mentor, might be to ask hard questions about yourself as a practitioner. We could consider:

- What is my role as a mentor?
- What is my practice like?
- Do I do a good job and if so how do I know?
- How has it my role developed since I began?
- What are the effects of my practice on the practitioners I mentor?
- How can I improve what I do?

Ghaye and Ghaye (1998), who have also written extensively about reflective practice, can take our questioning and thinking even further because they suggest that 'we can learn by talking to others about our practice, having it challenged, in a constructively critical manner …' (1998: 11).

This approach needs to take place in an open arena and be supported by a significant other (mentor) who has the experience and expertise to be an active listener. This puts us, as mentors, in the position of a practitioner being mentored and will further enhance our skills and qualities as a mentor. As a starting point we could share with colleagues:

- Our personal beliefs, values and understanding.
- Our theoretical understanding of early childhood and child development.
- The significant experiences that provided us with 'pauses for thought'.
- Our interpretation and conclusions from these experiences.
- Any new theories, ideas, policies and developments within the field.
- Our thoughts regarding our own personal and professional development.

Having considered ourselves as active reflective practitioners, we will be well placed to support the practitioners we mentor. It is then our responsibility as mentors to use strategies which include the posing of questions in order that our practitioners can be encouraged to reflect and move forward personally and professionally. Our own reflections will then, in part, need to focus in on the context in which our practitioner is working and learning. It is important for us as mentors to have an understanding of that context and also to realise that both the mentor and the practitioner must be open and willing to acknowledge that they can learn from each other and that it is not a hierarchical relationship (Neale, 2005).

As mentors we also need to become aware of any possible barriers or resistance to the reflective process. Chapter 2 considers the role of the mentor as being 'the one in the middle' and added to this are the difficulties we as mentors may believe a practitioner has in reflecting upon a particular issue, which could simply be due to a difference in understanding and thinking between us. We are then put into the position of 'scaffolding' the practitioner in a way that facilitates and enhances further reflective steps.

Teaching reflective practice

Having considered whether or not reflective practice is instinctive or intuitive and our position as reflective mentors we will now consider how reflective practice might be taught. The PiP project, referred to earlier, indicated that some practitioners in the quality early years settings studied within the project were supported in reflecting upon their practice by the researchers encouraging and working alongside them as role models (Blenkin and Kelly, 1997). This will in fact be the case where the mentor and practitioner are working regularly together but in some mentor–practitioner partnerships the mentor may visit the practitioner on an agreed day, for an agreed length of time and a negotiated purpose. Teaching by example becomes more problematic in this situation and the most has to be made of the 'visit times'. Some of the time may be spent observing the practitioner, with the remainder of the visit used for discussion and action planning. Within this there needs to be carefully considered questioning within the discussions in order to encourage reflection.

As mentioned above, it is important to remember that, as a mentor encouraging practitioners to reflect, they may sometimes be uncomfortable being asked about their opinions, since this is a new experience. Dadds (cited in Robins et al., 2003) points out that confronting and questioning practice, knowledge and understanding can sometimes cause significant discomfort for even the most experienced or qualified professionals. There is therefore a need for careful questioning, guidance and support in order to preserve self-esteem when we encourage reflection upon thoughts, understanding and practice. As a mentor we should be careful to provide encouragement and support by validating and confirming any emerging thinking with, at least initially, a minimum of evaluative feedback on the content of that thinking, as the practitioners resolve their own dilemmas. They often do not need answers, but rather opportunities to find their own.

Experience has taught us that, after any initial discomfort or uncertainty, reflection does become easier and can in fact be very enlightening. As mentioned earlier, in order for this point to be reached, support and encouragement by the mentor are needed. The support may come through one-to-one discussions with a practitioner or in a group discussion, with the practitioner as part of the group. It is through such discussions that thoughts values and ideas can be either confirmed or changed. In group situations, as confidence grows, so does respect for the ideas and experiences of others.

As suggested previously the teaching of reflective practice as a process should be surrounded by questions. Questioning, in the right way, will encourage a practitioner to reflect, and this questioning can begin by being quite basic.

Nutbrown (1994: 155) suggests the following questions which could be considered as an aid to the reflective process. These can be asked directly by you as a mentor or can be posed in such a way as to leave them with the practitioner to ponder and be revisited at your next meeting or discussion.

- Why did you/I do that?
- What made me/you do/say that?
- How shall you/I solve this?
- Who can you/I ask about that?

These questions are quite systematic in their ordering and as Dewey said:

> Reflection involves not simply a sequence of ideas, but a con-sequence – a consecutive ordering in such a way that each determines the next as its proper outcome, while each outcome in turn leans back on, or refers to, its predecessors. The successive portions of a reflective thought grow out of one another and support one another … .
>
> (Dewey 1933: 4)

An alternative list of questions that flow consecutively and link to one another could be taken from Brookfield (cited in Dryden *et al.*, 2005) who suggests four viewpoints from which to consider an 'event':

- Our own viewpoint.
- Our colleagues' viewpoints.
- The viewpoint of learners.
- The viewpoints offered by theoretical literature.

Again, using this list, questions can be asked and discussions held between you and your practitioner which will facilitate the reflective process.

A third approach is based on suggestions by Peters (cited in Dryden *et al.*, 2005: 4), who structures reflective thoughts around a Describing, Analysing, Theorising and Acting (DATA) cycle. This again could be a useful structure when teaching practitioners to reflect. It gives a starting point and then guides them through a reflective process step by step:

D Describe the problem, task or incident that needs to be looked at and possibly changed.
A Analyse the description, looking at assumptions that were made at the time and also any that are being made about how to respond now.
T Theorise about a range of ways to respond to the problem, task or incident.
A Act using one or more of the theories above.

The above lines of questioning may appear quite basic but they are systematic and the next thing to consider is: do they actually encourage the practitioner to think beyond the event in question? Do they actually challenge our practitioners to consider where they may go or what they might do next? This is a vital step in the reflection process because it is important that reflections on practice lead to effective changes being made. The DATA approach begins to do this in the theorising and acting stages.

A final set of questions that we may use when facilitating and teaching practitioners to reflect have slightly more detail to them. These will be preceded by a discussion about the actual 'event'.

- What new knowledge, ideas or skills have you taken from this session/training/experience/discussion?
- How might this impact upon your own thinking, values and/or practice within your setting or role?
- How might it impact upon the children with whom you/I work in terms of their learning and/or behaviour?
- What impact might it have on other colleagues or even parents/carers?
- What changes may it lead you to make to your practice?
- Is there any further training that could be undertaken that might enhance this new knowledge, ideas or skills?

It is through asking questions of significant learning experiences or pauses for thought moments that it should be possible to gain a greater understanding of personal and professional actions and thus improve practice.

Whichever questioning approach we, as mentors, choose to take we should ensure it is fit for the purpose and will allow the practitioner to develop their skills of reflection within a comfortable and supportive framework.

PRACTICAL SUGGESTIONS FOR MENTORS

Type a selection of questions or discussion starting points on to paper or card. Use them as a prompt for yourself during discussions with a practitioner or leave them with the practitioner to consider for themselves.

Reflective practice within an action–reflection cycle

Several writers concerned with reflective practice identify cyclical models of reflection which proceed through stages which include having an experience, reflecting on the experience, learning from the reflections and consequently making improvements to practice or changes in values and understanding.

Within one of the courses on which we teach, the Early Childhood HND at the University of Worcester, there is a requirement in a mandatory module for students to engage in research linked with reflection on their own experiences and professional development in the early years workplace. Students are taken through an action–reflection cycle, following which they are able to form a question which then leads them into an extended piece of research as an independent study.

Following experience within an early years setting, the students engage in a series of workshops which allow them time to undertake diary writing as a vehicle for reflection. These workshops also support their development of a research question and focus. The first workshop involves selecting a particular experience from practice and writing about it in their diary. Students are encouraged to write with as much detail as possible allowing themselves to 'relive' the incident. Out of these initial inconsequential but focused ramblings in their diaries the students begin to develop a more critically reflective approach to their experiences. As the tasks continue there begins to emerge more of a 'critical incident reflection' (Brown, 2000) approach. Further, collaborative peer and tutor–mentor discussion, develops the students' ability to shape their thoughts, the outcomes and the ability to pose further questions in order to move them forward in their thinking and understanding.

The accompanying case study is based upon an entry in a second-year early years HND diary. The writing contains reflection by a student /practitioner on an incident which took place in an early years setting in which she was employed.

CASE STUDY

Context
A member of staff was trying to manage a child's negative behaviour.

The experience
Adult. 'Billy, I would like you to say sorry to Amelia.'

Billy stands but turns to look the other way.

Adult. 'Billy, you really hurt Amelia.'

Billy still stands looking the other way and says, 'No.'

Adult. 'Oh, then I will just have to get Katherine, I wonder what she will say?'

The adult then walks over to me (Katherine) and explains the situation and asks me to deal with it. I talk to both the children, victim and culprit, listen to how they both feel and get them to try and sort it out themselves by thinking about what they could have done without hurting one another. The children gave each other a hug and walked away to play with someone else.

Reflection on the experience
Why did the adult need me to sort this problem out? Inside I felt they were using me as a threat to get the children to have positive behaviour. This was not the first time this situation had arisen. Regularly adults in my setting say to children, 'Oh, well! I shall have to get Katherine!' When these situations arise I feel angry that I am taken away from other children who need support. I keep my cool, as the children's feelings are more important, but I did air my views at a staff meeting, asking why they (other staff) did it. The reply was that children behave well only when I am around and they listen to me more. So why do children listen more to me? Why do children manage their behaviour effectively when situations arise after I have talked to them? Is there something else which is affecting the children and making them behave in a negative way? Do staff need to build their own confidence in managing negative behaviour instead of relying on me? Or is it me? Am I scary to the children and therefore they behave when they see me? Are children behaving like this to get my attention? And what happens when I am not around? How do the staff deal with behaviour management then?

Source: K. Moss (2003) Module 'Examining early childhood research' (part assessment for HND award).

Learning from reflection

Writing an account of the scene she witnessed enabled this student to start making sense not only of the interactions between children and children, adults and children and the adults' responses but also of working practices within the setting. Reliving the incident through the written word helped the student to question her own practice and that of others. She became more aware of not only the 'how' but the 'why' of practice.

Improvement of practice

Katherine began to make crucial links between theory and practice and through the asking of lots of questions identified where she could engage in further practitioner research with a view to changing practice, empowering herself and her colleagues and enriching the experiences of children.

> **CASE STUDY CONTINUED**
>
> *The outcome*
> A reflective outcome which became a research question for her subsequent independent study was articulated by the above student as: 'Are all day care practitioners effective managers of children's behaviour?'

Having told her story and reflected upon the experience by questioning it, her reflective writing certainly contains a voice which represents the processes within her thinking (Winter *et al.*, 1999) and that engaging in the reflective cycle 'changes something not quite fully understood … into something with more personal clarity, coherence and meaning' (Boud *et al.* in Ghaye *et al.* 1996).

The initial narrative process was painful for the student, who was wary of not writing 'academically'. She learned, as suggested by Bolton (2001), that you can't actually write the wrong thing and whatever you write will be right – for you. She soon became more confident in writing in this genre, which allowed her to 'live' her experience. As mentors we should enable our practitioners to experience this 'story-telling' and encourage them to see it as vital to the reflective process.

The next workshop encouraged a dialogue between the students in small groups which attempted to critically analyse each other's thoughts and ideas within their writing. Here Katherine was able to further make sense of the situation she had described and analysed.

The interaction with each other and with tutors/mentors who regarded reflective practice as a critical tool for analysing, evaluating and drawing out the consequences of actions following the student experiences supports our earlier suggestion that such conversations should examine, question and interpret practice critically in an open but supportive arena of active listening. Katherine became aware of the extent to which intuition had supported her reflections and also of the role that her diary writing played.

The role of reflective practice in improving quality and improving self

The quest for quality within the field of early childhood is high on the political and social programme and is embedded within *Every Child Matters* and the subsequent *Children's Workforce Strategy* (DfES, 2006) which sets out to 'build a world class workforce for children, young people and families' with a clear remit and intention to strengthen inter-agency and multi-disciplinary working. It can be said that a vision recognising development of practitioner skills as a core element requires practical approaches which include practitioners who are 'reflective' and who are supported by 'reflective' mentors. There is emphasis throughout these policies suggesting that part of the 'quality' in early years settings is to be found in the interaction of settings, practitioners, the children and their families.

Having identified these core issues we should now consider what we understand quality to be and its relationship with reflective practice.

PAUSE FOR THOUGHT

Professional development:

Consider the question 'What would be indicators of quality in an early years setting?' Using your own thoughts, conversation with peers, any reading you may have done and any evidence from a practice setting, bullet-point some ideas as a response to the above question.

As a response to the pause activity you may have considered the following as indicators of quality in an early years setting:

- Relations between children, staff and parents/carers and families.
- Staff qualifications and numbers.
- Behaviour.
- The ethos of the setting.
- Organisation of the environment.
- Group size.
- Activities of children.
- Child–adult interaction.

This list is by no means exhaustive and we should remember that quality will change over time and that it will also be viewed very differently from the perspectives of the children, their families and practitioners. If you were to ask families or the children the same question their answers might be quite enlightening.

To look at quality from a more theoretical perspective it could be described as 'a finite, static and mechanical idea, of a product which meets certain agreed and measurable criteria' (Penn 1994: 26). This definition of quality does serve a purpose in as much as it can set a minimum standard for achievement. It does not, however, serve the purpose of encouraging and perpetuating high expectations of provision and achievement that we consider throughout this chapter. The idea of quality as a dynamic process which evolves over time, as ever changing, collaborative and based on achievement of short- and long-term objectives is a more evaluative meaning of quality. Quality should be seen as context-related and also based upon value and healthy debate on these. Does this then give us a relationship between quality and reflective practice? We would say yes, because encountering different perspectives, thoughts and values suggests that practitioners are questioning their practice and thus entering into reflective practice in order to seek answers to questions which ultimately must benefit the individual and the group.

FINAL PAUSE FOR THOUGHT FOR MENTORS

Reflective practice and quality issues are interdependent because as suggested by Leeson (2004: 146): 'unless we engage in this process (of reflection), the work we do has the potential to be ill informed and possibly dangerous because we may perpetuate practice that is no longer relevant, simply because that is the way it has always been done and no one has questioned whether it is still appropriate'.

Critical skills of reflection are crucial to all workers in the field of early years, as the importance of insight and understanding will shape and form not only immediate practice but potentially the lives of children in our care and their families. Our role as reflective mentors, supporting and teaching reflective practitioners, is vital to the ongoing maintenance and development of quality provision in our early years settings.

Points to remember

The key issues that have been considered in this chapter are:

- Reflective thinking and reflective practice – what are they?
- Is reflective practice intuitive or instinctive?
- Mentors themselves as reflective practitioners
- Teaching reflective practice.
- Reflective practice within an action–reflection cycle.
- The role of reflective practice in improving quality and improving self.

📖 Further reading

Atkinson, T. and Claxton, G. (eds) (2000) *The Intuitive Practitioner: on the Value of not always Knowing what One is Doing.* Buckingham: Open University Press. This text explores the whole notion of intuition.

Dryden L., Forbes, R., Mukherji, P. and Pound, L. (eds) (2005) *Essential Early Years.* London: Hodder Arnold. Chapter 1 focuses on 'Launching into learning: becoming a reflective practitioner'.

Ghaye, A., and Ghaye, K. (1998) *Teaching and Learning through Critical Reflective Practice.* London: David Fulton. A more academic text which looks in depth at the importance and benefits of critical reflective practice.

Willan, J., Parker-Rees, R. and Savage, J. (eds) (2004) *Early Childhood Studies.* Exeter: Learning Matters. Contains a chapter written by C. Leeson, entitled 'In praise of reflective practice'.

4

Collecting and collating evidence through profiling

Victoria Eadie and Melanie Pilcher

The chapter begins by giving a definition of a profile as a tool for demonstrating professional practice and progression. It goes on to provide a framework for a profile whilst acknowledging the individuality of the task in terms of the way it demonstrates the uniqueness of the practitioner's own learning journey. The mentor and practitioner are guided through:

- A profiling exercise from start to finish.
- Generic evidence that can be found in any early years setting.
- Strategies for overcoming potential profiling problems.
- A case study of good practice in mentor support.
- The components of an exemplar profile contents and layout.
- An exploration of the mentor/practitioner roles and relationship during the profiling exercise.

What is a profile?

A profile or portfolio of evidence documents a practitioner's progression as they develop both professionally and personally as a result of studies or ongoing work-based practice. It shows first-hand how they relate theory to practice and allows contemporaneous reflection and evaluation to occur. It may be produced for the purposes of further or higher education, vocational training or as a personal record of a practitioner's self-development with no set criteria. Whether it is marked, assessed or simply created as a tool for reference by the individual, the profiling exercise takes the practitioner through a process of valuable self-expression. It should be mentioned that although this section focuses on the profile as an assessment tool, with set criteria, standards or learning outcomes to be met, it is equally relevant to the profile that is constructed as a personal diary or journal.

The term 'profile' is used throughout the chapter. A broader definition would have to include the reflective diary/journal, or log, as used in National Vocational Qualifications or by Higher Level Teaching Assistants, which may have a different emphasis in terms of content, but requires the same evaluative process to take place in order for it to be meaningful. The same could be said for anyone undertaking the profiling exercise; reflection and evaluation are the key components to its effectiveness, as discussed in Chapter 3. Above all else, recording and profiling enable the practitioner to measure previous learning experiences against newly discovered knowledge and understanding, which in turn facilitates new ways of thinking.

A profile also enables the practitioner to document evidence relating directly to their work practice, and demonstrates their practical skills as they are enhanced and refined through a reflective and evaluative process. The key elements of a profile or portfolio of evidence are that:

- It is primarily practitioner-led.
- It meets learning outcomes, personal and professional targets or a set of standards.
- It documents a 'learning journey'.
- It contains a range of evidence.
- It demonstrates continuous critical reflection and self-evaluation.

With the restrictions of academic writing conventions and prescriptive content of set assignments, a profile allows freedom of expression, offering an insight into the student as practitioner, or practitioner as reflective learner, which is sometimes difficult to capture. This is often further supported by direct observations and testimonies from colleagues within the workplace. A profile is no longer constructed simply for displaying pieces of work that prove one's abilities. Today's definition has expanded to include the practitioner's reflection and evaluation of the process, as well as reflecting on their methods and achievements; because of this, the profile or portfolio has become more common as a meaningful assessment tool in many vocational courses and in early years settings.

A good profile is a working document; its usefulness should continue long after any study is finished. It will contain valuable resources produced by the practitioner and is a record of activities undertaken, all of which demonstrate the practitioner's competence against a set of learning outcomes or personal and professional targets. It can be used to record continuing professional development or to illustrate the practitioner's career path to a prospective employer. Writers such as Fry *et al*. (1999) suggest that whilst portfolios or profiles are indeed becoming a more common means of demonstrating a practitioner's competence and professionalism we must be alert to the need for discrimination in evidence selection. The challenge is to make the best use of evidence that is readily available and fit for purpose. Consequently in order for a profile to be most effective the practitioner and mentor must have a shared understanding of what needs to be achieved, and both will need the confidence to select and agree upon appropriate evidence that meets any set criteria. There are, however, times when the profile may be a personal reflection of a particular learning journey and therefore is constructed autonomously without the need for criteria as these are set by the individual and are adapted as the journey progresses.

DISCUSSION POINT

Every profile is unique to the individual; it may take the form of a reflective diary or portfolio of evidence. It will contain a range of evidence, dictated to some extent by course learning outcomes, a set of standards or personal and professional targets. The mentor may make suggestions and at times agree the content of a profile, but its compilation and the types of evidence favoured must be practitioner-led.

How can the practitioner define the aims of their profile, why is this so important? How does the practitioner ensure that their aims for a profile complement the criteria or standards set?

Getting started

> Start by doing what is necessary, then do what is possible, and suddenly you are doing the impossible.
>
> St Francis of Assisi

With any practitioner-led activity there are barriers to getting started, some of which are self-imposed, others a result of outside influences, particularly when a profile is introduced at the start of an extended period of study. The same can also be true of those practitioners working in busy early years settings where simple day-to-day trials can delay the desire and the time for evidence collecting and reflectivity. Distant deadlines allow procrastination and motivation is often sidetracked by more immediate challenges.

A practitioner undertaking a college-based course may have concerns about the work load involved and their own capabilities. The role of the mentor in the early stages cannot be overestimated, especially in terms of making the profiling task seem like an exciting challenge. This important and sometimes complex practitioner–mentor relationship is explored in some detail in Chapter 2.

Being asked to compile a profile of evidence to be assessed or marked at some distant point in the future can imply an onerous task. Time scales should be implicit from the outset and one of the first challenges is to ensure that everyone involved understands their role and the aims and objectives of the profiling exercise. Those who need to be directly involved could include any of the following:

- The practitioner (as already discussed).
- The mentor.
- A critical friend or colleague.
- Course tutor/lecturer.
- An assessor.
- Employer/line manager.

Some of the above roles are interchangeable, for example the assessor or verifier is often the mentor and a mentor can adopt the role of 'critical friend' should the need arise.

The mentor will be an integral part of the profiling exercise from beginning to end. It is often assumed that they will possess all the skills required to nurture the practitioner through the process, but this is not always the case. The notion of a mentor being 'the one in the middle' is explored further in Chapter 3, but at the very least the mentor will require a whole repertoire of strategies to engage the adult learners in the task ahead and a good deal of 'self-awareness' in order to give credibility to their role.

A well defined set of roles and responsibilities avoids ambiguity. The possibilities of a mentor's role in the profiling process are identified below:

- To assist in the identification of evidence from taught programmes of study and/or work-based activities.
- To act as a link between all parties, the assessment centre, workplace, etc.
- To agree and, if required, sign off evidence.
- To set targets and ensure time scales are realistic and achievable.
- To offer suggestions for professional development activities.
- To check and monitor the progress of the profile at every stage, ensuring quality and parity throughout.
- To encourage self-evaluation and critical reflection within the profile.
- To visit and observe the practitioner within their workplace.
- To ensure that the critical friend understands their role and is empowered to support the practitioner.
- To promote a shared understanding of the profile as an assessment tool.
- To assist the practitioner in interpreting the learning outcomes and identification of appropriate evidence from taught modules and work based activities.
- To ask questions in order to teach, develop or facilitate reflective practice.

CASE STUDY

Setting an example

Annabel is mentor to a group of mature students who are required to compile a profile for the FdA EY. Students are told the purpose of the profile, when it should be completed, and who is involved in validating and signing off evidence. During taught sessions they look together at learning outcomes and criteria for the profile, the paperwork involved and the types of evidence that can be generated through work-based activities. Annabel will then support the students through the profiling task as part of her mentor role.

Despite being encouraged to concentrate on gathering evidence first and putting the profile together later, students still ask, 'What should my profile look like?' and 'How much evidence should go into it?' Annabel suggests they take the paperwork they have been given and put together a folder complete with headings and divisions, which will be ready for evidence to be added and claimed later. Many students are still hesitant, and are asking to see an example. Annabel decides to compile and collate a profile herself, complete with examples of evidence that meets the learning outcomes. She then claims the evidence and cross-references it accordingly. She now has an exemplar portfolio that can be shown to anybody who is involved in the process.

The case study demonstrates how the mentor gains a better understanding of the profiling task by undertaking the process. She then has a profile that could be used by other members of the mentoring or lecture team as a common framework to work towards with their own students or practitioners. The exemplar profile can also be used to enable the practitioner's workplace to gain a clearer understanding of what their colleague is trying to achieve; furthermore the practitioner now has something tangible to base their profile on and is no longer faced with the worry of 'getting it wrong'. Equally important is the sense of achievement and progress gained by setting the profile up in advance.

The components of an exemplar profile based upon that used in the case study are given in this chapter (see Box 4.1) and are offered, free of copyright, for reproduction and adaptation as required.

A Framework for the portfolio

When and how a profiling task is introduced to a practitioner will depend greatly upon the purpose for its development. It can be assumed that in a programme of study a profile will be longitudinal and that it will be introduced sooner rather than later, with a great deal of input from the mentor and/or course tutor. A suggested order for the various elements that may be within a profile will guide the practitioner in the early stages, and give consistency and flow to its overall development. It should be stressed that any such guidance must ultimately be dictated by what seems logical to the individual and will vary according to the requirements of the course or practitioner.

BOX 4.1

Suggested contents for a profile

- Contents list.

- Personal details and contacts.

- A *curriculum vitae*.

- Job description.

- Professional letters of recommendation.

- Personal statement of philosophy and values.

- Learning outcomes/overview of programme of study or standards (for example NVQ or HLTA or Early Years Professional).

- Record of progress.

- Marking or assessment criteria.

- Observation plans.

- Record of mentor observations, visits, discussions and feedback.

- Evidence of peer/colleague support.

- Record of discussions with an academic personal tutor or assessor.

- Actual evidence.

Whatever the purpose of the profile, at least three distinct processes will take place as it is put together, all of which are the responsibility of the practitioner, but involve support from the mentor. The process begins with the practitioner and mentor deciding what constitutes 'evidence' for the purpose of the profiling exercise. Once this is established the compilation of the profile begins, albeit somewhat loosely at this point. Finally the evidence is put to work as it is evaluated and reflected upon ready for presentation. A well structured framework supports these stages, allowing the practitioner to concentrate instead upon the task of evidence gathering. It is important to note it is part of a cyclical process and should be revisited at any time by both the practitioner and the mentor.

Identifying and gathering evidence

Types of evidence

Before considering the types of evidence that a profile might contain, it is important to consider what is meant by 'evidence' in an early years setting. Any task or work produced as part of the practitioner's role or in pursuit of professional development is potential evidence provided it can be confirmed or corroborated in some way. The practitioner compiling a profile will be doing so to meet a set of learning outcomes or standards that demonstrate their ability to meet such criteria, in other words the evidence is the facts that support their work-based practice. The evidence contained in the profile will have been selected because it demonstrates occupational competence. Broadly speaking, evidence can take many forms provided the practitioner and mentor are satisfied that it is authentic – generated by the practitioner, valid – linking to a set of standards or learning outcomes, and current – demonstrating the practitioner's knowledge of government initiatives and contemporaneous issues. Currency is a particularly exciting challenge for those working in a sector where change is inevitable as policy makers continually strive to achieve better outcomes for children.

When confronted with the mission of identifying and gathering evidence, the practitioner may feel that they are faced with an overwhelming task, indeed some will not know where to begin, and will require a good deal of support from the mentor. Even so, the mentor must be mindful that the support they offer does not stifle the self-expression that is central to the whole process. A balance must be struck between the type and amount of material being placed in the profile and keeping it manageable. Without some form of regulation a profile can quickly become cumbersome as an unconfident practitioner crams everything in 'just to be on the safe side'.

Whilst it is imperative that guidance is offered, the question remains as to what form it should take. One solution is to produce guidance for evidence that should be, in the main, readily available for the practitioner to gather at their setting. When giving out such a list it is important to stress that it is not prescriptive but merely a starting point from which to launch the profile. (This will allay any worries if a particular evidence type is not available at a setting.) It is vital that the practitioner and mentor discuss the suitability of evidence and the opportunities that may generate it.

Box 4.2 contains examples of generic evidence suitable for a range of purposes. It is by no means exhaustive; the intent is to provide a mentor and practitioner with a basis for thought, discussion and exploration of further possibilities.

BOX 4.2

Sources of evidence

Planning
annotated, for example in order to indicate the level of practitioner involvement in the delivery of an activity or session, or their thoughts and reflections on the process.

Individual play, behaviour or education plans
clearly identifying the level of practitioner involvement in their writing and implementation.

Photographs
of practitioner-instigated displays/friezes and images of activities as they are taking place. Protecting the identity of the children is of paramount importance and there should be clear evidence of written permission from parents when necessary. Photographs are particularly useful where there is no written or pictorial evidence available.

BOX 4.2 continued

Print or photocopies
may include computer-generated work, children's work from books, ex-display work and examples of emergent writing. Planning, records and letters written to other agencies may also be used, reproduced within the boundaries of confidentiality and data protection.

Information sharing
within the practitioner's remit this may include accounts of working with integrated services and other agencies involved with their organisation.

Child observations
that inform a child's learning and development, Early Years Foundation Stage or Child Concern models. All of which allow valuable reflection and evaluation to take place as the practitioner identifies the impact their practice has upon children in their care.

Observations
of the practitioner undertaking tasks and activities, usually conducted by a mentor or colleague; may be planned or incidental.

Consultations and interviews
with children, parents, colleagues and other agencies; carried out by the practitioner and recorded as reflective accounts or reports.

Minutes
of meetings attended that identify actions arising for which the practitioner has responsibility and which are supplemented by their own notes from the meeting.

Trips and outings
Details of any organised by the practitioner, supported by photographs and documentation.

Festivals/celebrations/collective worship
Class/group assemblies planned and carried out by the practitioner. Evidence of how a setting values difference, diversity and the needs of others.

Out-of-school care or clubs
A practitioner may have additional duties or sole responsibility through involvement with an extended school or other provider.

Training and courses
photocopied certificates of training attended (the mentor may want to validate the originals) or training materials produced by the practitioner for dissemination to others.

Inclusion
Can the practitioner show evidence of how they make sure that activities or lessons are inclusive for all children and how they differentiate for those with special needs?

BOX 4.2 continued

Team player
Collaborative working and evidence of collective tasks or projects undertaken. Can the practitioner identify the skills that make them effective team members?

Parental involvement
The practitioner could use examples of their involvement in strategies for involving parents in their child's learning and development – from simple exchanges of information to parents' evenings.

SWOT analysis (strengths, weaknesses, opportunities and threats)
undertaken at regular intervals, identifying strategies for personal and professional development.

Supplementary diary or journal
Experiences and incidents can be recorded regularly, allowing interpretation of their significance as they are linked with learning outcomes or criteria within the profile at a later date.

The practitioner and mentor must be aware that evidence gathering will be time-consuming and may have an impact on colleagues; therefore support from others is particularly important at this stage. Colleagues may be protective over their work and feel pressured by the practitioner who wants to critically evaluate tasks they have carried out together. Mentor visits to the workplace can help to alleviate this if they allocate time to talk to everyone involved, share information and give reassurance that the evidence is being used appropriately.

Mentors' confidence in making suggestions

Evidence gathering is of course fundamental to a profile. However, in order for mentors to have confidence in making suggestions that assist practitioners in the compilation of their profiles and making best use of the evidence, it is necessary for them to possess a comprehensive knowledge base; Stephenson and Lehmann (1995) draw attention to the importance of this in-depth knowledge base by discussing the fact that all mentors need to be well informed in a variety of academic disciplines as well as having professional expertise. They go on to suggest that they must have a variety of approaches to involve practitioners; this is equally important whether the profiling task is self-directed or being undertaken as part of a course or programme of study. There will inevitably be an academic element to the profile that some practitioners will need more support with than others: it will depend greatly on their past experience of higher or further education. The mentor will be required to suggest strategies for research, curriculum planning or critiquing skills among other things and should have competence in these areas too.

It can also be argued that a mentor cannot have confidence making suggestions if they themselves have not had the same or very similar experiences to those they are supporting. Through the knowledge base they possess and their work-based experiences mentors are well equipped to make suggestions. However, it needs to be stressed that a fundamental part of confidence is self-belief and it is this that comes with experience of the process and trusting in your own judgement.

A crucial aspect of the profile is that it shows professional development and progression throughout. Opportunities for professional development are to be found by attending training or workshops, conducting research, taking on new roles and responsibilities or disseminating information to colleagues – in fact any activity that increases one's vocational knowledge and understanding provided it is identified by the practitioner and, as such, is reflected upon.

PAUSE FOR THOUGHT

The mentor must encourage the practitioner to date and annotate everything as it is collected. Even in the early stages the practitioner should attempt to link evidence to appropriate learning objectives or standards and begin collation in readiness for it to be claimed within the profile. A simple index of the evidence as it is collected will be invaluable, allowing the practitioner to identify any gaps in plenty of time to source other data.

With the task of evidence gathering established, the practitioner will devise their own methods for it to be safely stored until they are ready to claim it within a profile. The mentor should be prepared to view evidence at any stage in order to ensure that the practitioner understands the task and is making good progress. This practice is of vital importance, as regular formative feedback can buoy confidence (of both the practitioner and the mentor) and assist the appropriate development of the profile.

Once evidence collection has commenced, initial worries and concerns usually disperse, and a new issue takes over: 'What do I do with it now?'

Collating evidence

For some, the process of filing and claiming evidence within a profile will begin almost immediately; others will wait until they have collected a significant amount before doing so. Either way is fine, as long as the mentor has the opportunity to view the evidence and discuss it at regular intervals.

Whatever the structure or purpose of the profile, occasionally it will be necessary to leave the organisation of certain pieces until the profile is nearing completion. Through leaving evidence practitioners can later place it where there may be 'gaps' in their profile (if it meets the necessary criterion for that particular section). What is important is that evidence is claimed in the right place within a profile, remembering that this will not always be where the mentor thinks it should be, but where it seems most logical for the practitioner to place it.

Some will prefer to keep their evidence together at the back of their profile, cross-referencing to several learning outcomes, criteria or standards; others will want to place it in sections according to the learning outcomes or standards – maintaining a 'one piece of evidence to one learning outcome/standard' approach, especially those who find cross-referencing time-consuming and complicated. It is very difficult to impose a system of cross-referencing on somebody when the profiling task is encouraged as a practitioner-led process. If this is the case, the mentor must offer suggestions and advice whilst letting the practitioner maintain control. Once again, the criteria for the profile as discussed later in this chapter hold the key to accurate and appropriate organisation; the need for the practitioner to understand the criteria is paramount.

As evidence gathering progresses a new challenge presents itself. Linking evidence to learning outcomes or standards is all very well, but, as we have already identified, reflection and evaluation are integral to the profiling process and are the key to turning ordinary experiences into the critical incidents that make the evidence work.

Any evidence has the potential to become a critical incident when reflection and evaluation take place; at the very least, the mentor should be able to see that the evidence claimed links with certain learning outcomes or standards. The question may well arise as to how and where exactly the reflection and evaluation take place within a profile. A separate form or 'front sheet' filed with each piece of evidence, as used in the exemplar profile mentioned earlier (Box 4.1, p. 51), is one suggestion. It will assist both the practitioner and the mentor in ensuring that the reflection and evaluation have taken place by giving some structure to the process. The reflective activity based on pieces of evidence or critical incidents can also be supported by discussions between the practitioner and mentor based on questioning as outlined in Chapter 3.

The contents of a 'front sheet' will differ according to the requirements of the profile and the practitioner; National Vocational Qualifications (NVQs) in particular are structured to facilitate this process. However, for some other courses a front sheet will:

- Ensure that every piece of evidence is evaluated and reflected upon by providing somewhere for it to be recorded.
- Clearly link evidence with the learning outcomes and taught modules or standards.
- Give evidence a title and clear focus.
- Allow the mentor, practitioner and other members of the assessment team to identify the learning that has taken place.
- Develop links between learning and practice.
- Aid the target setting and planning process.

It is imperative that if a front sheet is to be used, the practitioner understands exactly what they are being asked to do and why. Through both written and verbal feedback from the mentor, practitioners can be given suggestions as to how they might structure their own version, encouraging ownership of the process. The use of a front sheet for evidence also provides a strong element of quality within a profile, along with a method of formative assessment and evidence of academic progress linked directly with practice. It is also important to note that a front sheet and the associated evidence should be seen as work in progress and may be annotated and developed at any time throughout the life of the profile. This enables reflection and evaluation to take their purest form. Figure 4.1 is one example of a front sheet that may be copied for general use.

Troubleshooting (quality rather than quantity)

Anyone involved in the process of evidence gathering (either mentor or assessor) will invariably find that they are presented with two extreme groups, those whose profiles bulge with evidence and those who have collected the absolute minimum amount.

One important point to highlight is that the number of pieces of evidence can be somewhat irrelevant, as it is the quality rather than the quantity that counts. It is inevitably the practitioner who lacks confidence or understanding of the process who will over-compensate by filling their profile with cursory pieces of work that link tenuously (if at all) with the profile criteria. The mentor then faces the challenge of encouraging them to discard some pieces in order to maintain validity. It is occasionally necessary to compromise and allow evidence to stay, provided it is further supported by other pieces, if there is sufficient capacity within the profile to do so.

Conversely those practitioners whose profile is lacking need to ensure that they have sufficient evidence within it to meet the profile criteria. Some will require more directed activities in the early stages whereby the mentor gives clear instructions as to exactly what can be done to achieve the learning outcomes or standards. There should be no problem with the mentor taking such a prescriptive stance, provided they are aware of when and how to place the responsibility back with their practitioner in order that they are able to develop both professionally and academically. Chapter 2 discusses the challenge of handling such a situation with the sensitivity needed, acknowledging that it is a crucial requirement in order to maintain a successful mentor–practitioner relationship.

Exemplar evidence front sheet

Evidence No:

Evidence title . . . .

Date of evidence . . . .

Type of evidence . . . .

Learning outcomes / Criteria / Standards covered . . . . . .

Links to . . . .

Evaluation and reflection

Figure 4.1 Example of an evidence front sheet.

Occasionally, negative feedback has to be given but the mentor must remember that even a profile that appears to be failing in its purpose still represents a lot of time and effort on the part of the practitioner, and, whilst it is imperative that they respond to the mentor's advice, the way it is communicated will be of the essence.

The practitioner who leaves everything until the last minute will require similarly sensitive handling, combined with a more directed approach. Deadlines must be negotiated with all parties, ensuring that the practitioner retains control over the task ahead, whilst enabling the mentor to intervene when appropriate, allowing plenty of time for problems to be addressed. Some thought must also be given to the individual's method of working. A last-minute approach suits some people, but for others it would be disastrous to let them get that far behind with their work.

DISCUSSION POINTS

Does the practitioner anticipate problems accessing or generating certain types of evidence? If so, have they identified a sufficient range to cover the learning outcomes or standards comprehensively? What support do they think they require from the mentor in order to keep them on track? Are expectations of the level of mentor support available to them realistic? What are the possible strategies that the mentor and practitioner agree will work for them if problems should arise?

Signing off evidence and marking the profile

By the time a profile is 'complete' the mentor should be familiar with its content and the practitioner's style of evidence presentation. Individual pieces of evidence will have been agreed or signed off over the duration of the task, indicating that the mentor or academic tutor agrees that they meet the required criteria of the profile. When complete the profile should be looked at holistically, remembering that it is the sum of all its parts. Weaker evidence can be 'shored up' by stronger examples provided professional development is evident. In some cases the evidence may be weak but the actual reflection and evaluation detailed and enlightening.

If a profile is used or graded as a piece of academic work within a programme of study it is important to ensure that there are criteria the mentor adheres to in order to assist the assessment process. Fry *et al.* (1999: 224) specify the need for 'clear and open criteria' and 'a specified structure' to assist in making profiles a 'fairer method of assessment'.

By having guidelines to work to, the mentor will feel more confident in making a judgement. However, owing to the very nature of a profile it is individual to the practitioner, and any criteria must be designed to fit the whole range and ultimate purpose of the profile. It must be acknowledged that producing assessment criteria that meet these needs fairly and are consistently acceptable across a wide range is indeed a challenge.

Supporting the collation of evidence for the practitioner's profile

It is this variation of profiles which can result in the signing off or marking becoming a time-consuming task; obviously the larger the cohort or group the longer this process will take. The task must not be underestimated. It can take a long time to assess or grade profiles; it also requires confidence and self-belief on the part of the mentor, relevant vocational knowledge and a set of clear criteria to guide the process. It is also important from the point of validity and reliability that there is an effective verification procedure, so that both students and mentors are supplied with reassurance of quality and fairness that do not restrict the individuality of the profile.

A good baseline for a completed profile would be that it is well organised and clearly cross-referenced in the practitioner's preferred style. It uses evidence that demonstrates knowledge, values and skills which underpin the practitioner's development and which are evaluated and reflected upon throughout. It must demonstrate an understanding of difference and diversity and of course maintain confidentiality as appropriate within the evidence used.

A profile should be considered complete only when the practitioner and mentor feel that they have satisfactorily covered the learning outcomes or standards with a range of evidence that is fit for the purpose. It could also be assumed that it will probably demonstrate:

- Satisfactory reports from those involved in the assessment process.
- Evidence of follow-up on actions identified by the mentor and others.
- Explicit links within reflective evidence to the learning that has taken place.
- Clear links between evidence and the professional and practical skills required for the course or programme of study being undertaken.

The most important criteria for a finished profile would have to be that the practitioner feels a sense of achievement. Equally important would be that the reflection and evaluative processes embedded within the profiling task have become second nature as their value becomes clear.

PAUSE FOR THOUGHT

The completion of a profile is not the end of the story. The mentor should be asking the practitioner to reflect upon the profile building exercise. What has been learnt from the process? How will the practitioner continue to implement the skills they have developed? Will they revisit the profile in the future?

Points to remember

The challenge of writing a chapter concerning evidence gathering and profiling is compounded by the range of reasons for doing so. The authors have drawn heavily upon their personal experience in developing support materials for the FdA EY whilst maintaining a generic focus within the field of early years.

- Compiling a profile of evidence is at first a daunting task but through the expert support of mentors and/or assessors it should be a process of both personal and professional development.
- It is an opportunity for the practitioner to learn more about themselves and the way in which they work, a chance to celebrate achievements and learn from disappointments in a manner that is recorded for future use. (This is true for both practitioner and mentor.)
- Whilst this chapter focuses on the profile as a tool of assessment by others, supported by someone undertaking the role of a mentor, we have ensured that the personal diary or journal is given equal credence.
- Whatever form it takes, an effective profile is to be shared with others, to 'show off' talents and to inform future practice.

Further reading

Brown, S., Race, P. and Smith, B. (1996) *Assessing Student Learning in Higher Education*. London: Routledge. A useful book on assessment which contains helpful guidance on the marking of profiles/portfolios, as well as other areas of assessment.

Moon, J. (1999) *Reflection in Learning and Professional Development*. London: Kogan Page. This book provides an insight into understanding and using reflection to enhance learning in practice and would be useful for both mentor and practitioner.

Website

http://www.siue.edu/assessment/portf.html An American website which discusses the use of portfolios

5

Designing and implementing a mentoring scheme
University of Worcester SureStart-recognised sector-endorsed Foundation Degree in Early Years
Janet Murray

This chapter identifies the principles underpinning the design of a mentoring scheme for early years practitioners seeking Senior Practitioner status through the SureStart-recognised Sector-endorsed Foundation Degree in Early Years (FdA EY). A case study of the mentoring scheme implemented by the University of Worcester (UW) is discussed, with issues of application and effectiveness drawn out for readers to consider and relate to their own context.

UW delivers the foundation degree through five partner colleges of further education and, since 2005, in a children's centre in collaboration with an Early Years Development and Childcare Partnership (EYDCP).

First principles

Collaborative and reflective learning is at the heart of professional development in the early years sector because it suits the professional nature of working with young children and complements the pedagogical approach to developing young children as learners. In early years pedagogy children are encouraged to play a major part in constructing their own learning through talk, exploration and discovery, social interactions with their peers and setting their own challenge. This active engagement in their own learning requires a supportive framework which is provided by the adult professional to enable the child to advance its learning and development. These pedagogical principles are based on the theory that learning is socially constructed and that 'human learning presupposes a specific social nature' (Vygotsky, 1978: 88). These ideas are applicable to adult learning, particularly in the context of mentoring adults to promote professional learning in the early years. It seems highly appropriate, therefore, to translate pedagogy into andragogy (adult learning principles) through a mentoring system. 'Andragogy works best in practice when it is adapted to fit the uniqueness of the learners and the learning situation' (Knowles *et al.*,1998: 3).

The mentoring system adopted by UW for the FdA EY was designed as a fusion of early years pedagogy with andragogy, to provide a tailor-made approach to practice-based learning, which is relevant to the sector. A tiered system of mentoring was devised which incorporated and reflected pedagogical and andragogical principles, combining peer support in the workplace (professional critical friend) with a visiting professional mentor (practice mentor), all working within a framework for guiding the individual development of the practitioner (early years profile).

Reflecting the principles in the design

Knowles et al. (1998) argue that the core principles of andragogy are applicable to all adult learning situations provided the design considers differences in the situation, the individual and the nature of the subject. Andragogy is focused on the characteristics of adult learning rather than a specific set of goals. It is based on the belief that adult learning takes place through interactions and situations. Mentoring is, therefore, a highly appropriate approach to use in supporting adult learning in the workplace because its principal function is to facilitate the process of experiential learning, enabling the learner to draw personal meaning and value from significant experience within their specific context or situation. The aim of the mentoring system in the FdA EY is to support the practitioner in practice-based learning for professional development directed towards the achievement of professional and practical skills.

It will be a strength in any early years mentoring system if it allows appreciation of the learner's unique context and makes use of situational factors to further the most immediate and relevant areas for development and change. The design and structure of the mentoring system will need to provide the means to heighten the learner's awareness of significant experience as it occurs and opportunity to reflect afterwards, so that they can capitalise on this personally, and share with colleagues in the particular context of the workplace. Access to support in the workplace from a more competent peer can be invaluable in this respect by providing timely support and recognition of learning opportunities as they occur. Thus the *Professional Critical Friend* (PCF) was a role identified in the Worcester mentoring scheme to provide front-line peer support and to assure fuller appreciation of the workplace context and the learner's situation within it (Box 5.1).

BOX 5.1

Worcester mentoring system: role descriptors

Professional Critical Friend

Aim: to provide regular and ongoing feedback on practice as a critical but supportive colleague.

Role: the Critical Friend will:

- Provide direct support for learning in the workplace by meeting learners at least once a fortnight to support reflection, ongoing progress evaluation and action planning.

- Undertake observations of the learner at least once a month, on the basis of action identified by the learner and agreed in the fortnightly meetings (or from tutorials with academic tutor/practice mentor).

- Liaise with the practice mentor/academic tutor.

- Provide practical support for the learner in the workplace in the fulfilment of the foundation degree.

- Attend an annual meeting (one day training) organised by the university or partner college.

The Professional Critical Friend is unpaid and normally a colleague identified in the workplace. It could be:

- A peer practitioner with at least equivalent qualifications and five years' relevant experience.

- A line manager.

This role is intended to provide largely informal and immediately available local support, which could also encourage the development of a mutually beneficial peer learning culture within the workplace. The involvement of a more experienced peer within the workplace provides the blend of pedagogical and andragogical principles referred to earlier by offering scope for shared construction of learning through regular dialogue, reflection and action.

Finding appropriate critical friends in the workplace, however, can be difficult, particularly in situations where the practitioner is the senior person in the organisation. The requirement for a critical friend who is more experienced and at least equally qualified limits the potential candidates in some early years settings and thus it is quite likely that the only person fitting the criteria is also the practitioner's line manager. Whilst there could be advantages in strengthening the manager's involvement and understanding, it could compromise the informal nature of the critical friend's role. Alternatively it might change the role into more of a coaching model, which some practitioners might prefer. Consequently the Worcester scheme built in flexibility and gave practitioners the opportunity to identify their own critical friend (PCF) within guidelines regarding an 'appropriate' person. It is suggested that choosing your mentor can have advantages, provided the choice is guided by limited options or against criteria. In settings where no critical friend can be easily identified, local professional networks or fellow practitioner-students can be useful alternatives.

Informal mentoring has the advantage of building on existing relationships as well as immediacy of access and local knowledge but access to the professional expertise of trained mentors, external to the early years setting, also has a role in providing more holistic, personal support to develop skills in reflection and capitalise on the wider learning opportunities. 'A formal structure is essential because it provides meaning and direction for relationships and support where necessary' (Clutterbuck, 2004: 28).

A *practice mentor* role was therefore devised to fulfil this function and provide a professional link between the practitioner, the employer and the college tutor or course provider (Box 5.2). This combination of the more informal role of the PCF with the externally appointed Practice Mentor (PM) is intended to blend and balance the formal and informal mentoring elements for the practitioner whilst engaging essential stakeholders (employer, college/course provider and the professional sector) in meaningful involvement in the mentoring process. The PM plays a key role as 'the one in the middle', mediating and liaising between all participants involved in practice-based learning, i.e. the practitioner-student, the employer, the critical friend, the course tutor and fellow mentors.

BOX 5.2

Worcester mentoring system: role descriptors

Practice Mentor
Aim: to provide professional support and guidance for work-based learning and professional development.

Role: the Practice Mentor will:

- Undertake observations of the learner, authenticating their practice and encouraging reflection on practice (three visits annually).

- Support the learner (and critical friend) in keeping up to date with professional developments.

- Contribute to the assessment of the work-based element of the award by verifying records and reports in the learner's record of achievement/professional practice profile (EY profile).

- Liaise with the employer/professional critical friend in reviewing the learner's progress.

- Guide the learner with work-based assessment evidence.

- Liaise with the academic tutor and provide a report on the learner's progress (three times a year visit reports).

- Attend one annual meeting organised by the university for mentoring and quality monitoring.

BOX 5.2 continued

The Practice Mentor is appointed and paid by the university/partner and could be:

- A practitioner with mentor training.
- LEA advisory/link teacher or mentor teacher.
- Higher or further education tutor with relevant professional background.

Professional mentors visiting an organisation can be invaluable in providing confidential, individual support for the practitioner but this requires time for relationship building and the development of trust with both the practitioner and the employer. The PM has to be seen as someone committed to the development of the practitioner within the organisation for this trust to develop. The external position and dual functions of the PM, as supporter and evaluator, can create tension in the way the role is perceived by the organisation and the practitioner. This tension can be eased if the dual functions are set clearly within a shared commitment to quality improvement and recognition of the potential value of practice-based learning to overall quality enhancement. The tension is also eased by the emphasis on self-evaluation and personal development planning against known criteria. The medium for this, in the FdA EY, is the Early Years Profile (EYP), which sets out the criteria for professional and practical skills against which the practitioner self-evaluates and plans personal development action. The profile is the shared focus of mentoring support from both the PCF and the PM, providing a vehicle for dialogue and supporting common understandings of expectations and interpretations of criteria.

The value of practice-based learning

Practice-based learning makes a fundamental contribution to real achievement and transformation in the early years professional context. Successful mentoring recognises its potential value by enabling the practitioner to make the most of the rich experiential learning resource which is the workplace. There is potential for new insights to emerge from discussion and analysis of practice in relation to the direct application of theory, within the specific workplace context. By guiding analysis of significant experience, the mentor is raising the practitioner's awareness of their ways of thinking and acting, enabling perspective transformation and 'critical reflectivity' (Mezirow, 1985, Brookfield, 1986, cited in Knowles et al., 1998: 105). The mentor acts as a guide to help the practitioner make sense of their individual context and to aid evaluation of their own skills, knowledge and attitudes in order to develop and grow in competence.

Discussion between practitioner and professional critical friend

Mentoring is a means of capability building for the practitioner, which should, in turn, have beneficial outcomes for the immediate workplace and potentially the wider sector through fulfilment of individual potential and dissemination of practice. The mentoring system should facilitate the practitioner to make a difference, gain value personally, professionally, and contribute to service quality and improvements. Verified evidence of changes and transformation taking place will demonstrate the impact of practice-based learning and the effectiveness of the mentoring system. Statements of professional standards can be useful as a measure of performance but need to involve multiple perspectives for effective application, reflection and evaluation. Self-evaluation is central but is supported in critical reflectivity if it is complemented by the expertise of other professional 'witnesses'. A tiered mentoring system is useful in this respect, offering insights from the workplace through the PCF and complemented by the external professional perspective of the PM. It is further prompted and developed by opportunities to discuss and share reflections with other practitioner-students. In the FdA EY, weekly discussion groups are led by an academic tutor and focus on practice-based learning and the EYP, offering a forum for dialogue, evaluation and dissemination of practice. Bolton (2001: 4) defines reflective practice as 'a process of learning and developing through examining our own practice, opening our practice to scrutiny by others, and studying texts from the wider sphere'.

Thus the structure of a mentoring scheme to support reflective practice needs to create opportunities for these elements to be incorporated and interconnected through interactions at different levels (see Figure 5.1).

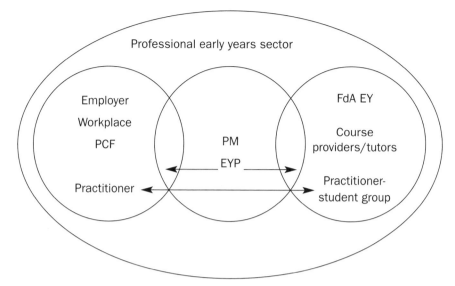

PM Practice Mentor, PCF Professional Critical Friend, EYP Early Years Profile, FdA EY Foundation degree in early years

Figure 5.1   Interactions within the FdA EY mentoring scheme: developing a learning community.

Attaching academic credit to the learning evidenced in practice recognises and signifies its value. It is an acknowledgement of learning as a process of change and development in knowledge, skills and attitudes which takes place over time. Consequently, mentoring support for the process also needs to be sustained over a sufficient period for transformation to emerge. Professional development courses with practice-based elements supported by mentoring will need to allow sufficient continuity of experience prior to assessment and periodic formative feedback on which the practitioner and mentor can build. The Worcester mentoring scheme was designed as a supportive arm within the course assessment framework, guiding the collection of evidence from practice for the EYP. This constitutes the assignment for work-based modules which span each year and level of study. Thus the practitioner-student builds up a continuous developmental profile of evidence of professional and practical skills, emerging competences, reflections and insights with periodic requirements to incorporate feedback from mentors and self-re-evaluation to monitor progress and achievement.

Developing a learning community

Individual learning in and from practice is not the only or ultimate goal of a mentoring system and it would have limited value if the benefits stopped there. Conversations between the practitioner, employer and mentors open up opportunities for individual learning to be applied to the wider organisation.

Also, each practitioner brings their workplace learning to group tutorials and discussions in college, developing and sharing their insights through dialogue. Although the professional expertise of the PM is primarily focused on individual support, the role has wider implications and potential impact through the relationship with the PCF and employer, the course tutors and fellow mentors. Time and opportunity for the PM to develop these relationships and obtain feedback is central to monitoring the effectiveness of the programme and also for promoting reinvestment of learning in quality enhancement and improvement of practice. The PM can act as a conduit for communication and dissemination, so that the benefits gained go beyond the individual. Adult education can be a means to further personal and organisational aims and goals and facilitate more synergy between the two to achieve complementarity rather than conflict. The practitioner benefits from a better understanding of the organisation and their motivation within it; the organisation benefits from the enhanced performance and motivation of the practitioner. A drawback in the early years sector is the lack of tangible reward and recognition of benefit in pay and promotion prospects.

In principle, however, a tiered mentoring system can provide the potential for wider benefits and dissemination of learning through the different levels of interaction:

• In the workplace, between the practitioner, PCF, employer and PM.
• In the college/course provider, between fellow practitioner-students, tutors and PMs.
• In the wider professional context of the PMs visiting multiple early years settings.

In order to maximise the potential benefits from these interactions, opportunities need to be available for purposeful involvement of all the different stakeholders in identifying and evaluating achievements and a means to feedback and share these. Thus a cycle of learning can arise from interactions related to the mentoring function and lead to the fostering of a learning culture and the development of a learning community (see Figure 5.1). MacNaughton (2003: 271) defines a learning community as 'an association of individuals, groups and organisations that evolves or develops as a whole through learning, rather as a living organism does'.

The practicalities

Not only does the design of a mentoring system need to fit the purpose and philosophy of the professional learning intentions, it also has to be feasible, practical, manageable, affordable, and meet any sector or equivalent requirements. (This was the Statement of Requirement (DfES, 2001) in the case of the FdA EY.) It is vital, therefore, to take the earliest opportunity, preferably in the design stage, to consult and involve the stakeholders in the sector and those instrumental to its implementation and on whom it may be dependent for its

---

KEY PRINCIPLES IN THE DESIGN OF AN EARLY YEARS MENTORING SYSTEM

- Peer support in the workplace through a chosen critical friend.

- A framework of professional mentor support.

- Recognition of the uniqueness of the learner and their situation.

- Time for relationship building.

- A common vehicle for promoting, recording and assessing development.

- A framework for dialogue, communication and interaction.

- Tangible value and accreditation for practice-based learning.

- A point of liaison and integration between all parties.

- Promotion of a learning culture and community.

---

eventual success. In the example of the Worcester mentoring scheme, consultation with employers, LEA adviser/inspectors and EYDCPs early in the design stage permitted practical factors to be considered and potential pitfalls to be avoided. The direct input of sector knowledge was invaluable but soon revealed the economic realities of partnership and the difficulties of drawing on sector expertise for mentoring where there was no financial provision to make this practicable. Sector endorsement was not backed up with the financial means to offer professional mentoring support. Affordability remains a key issue.

Any mentoring system needs to be robust and sustainable, with a ready supply of appropriately qualified and experienced mentors who can be remunerated within the funds available. Minimum criteria for the appointment of practice mentors were identified to assure a baseline for quality but which would still yield a reasonable supply. The validation of a Postgraduate Certificate in Early Years Mentoring by UW offered mentors further professional development and a means of capitalising on the learning gained from fulfilling the role. It also created a pool of experts to 'mentor the mentors'. A mentoring group was established to provide a forum for mentors and course leaders to share their experiences and evaluate and develop the mentoring function. Initially it provided a forum for clarifying and expanding the mentoring roles outlined in the original course documentation and developing shared understandings of the different functions in practice. Their meetings provide a problem-sharing and -solving opportunity and a communication channel to integrate the workplace and college perspectives. The value of such a forum has been evident in the production of a mentoring guide arising from reflection on their combined experiences over eighteen months of involvement in the Worcester FdA EY mentoring scheme. This bears out Clutterbuck's statement that 'Meetings between mentors to develop their skills can become informal, self-driven support networks' (Clutterbuck, 2004: 29).

The mentoring group has provided a supportive network for inducting, promoting, sustaining and developing the mentoring system. The next step is to offer training, professional development and qualifications in recognition of the role of the PCFs, who remain informal, unpaid mentors but who could hold the key to developing a learning culture in early years settings through mentoring in the workplace.

KEY POINTS

The practicalities

- Affordability: funding the mentoring system.

- Availability and quality of critical friends/mentors.

- Support, training and accreditation for critical friends/mentors (informal/formal systems).

- Obtaining and sustaining sector involvement.

- Promoting and sustaining a mentoring culture.

Impact: more than the sum of its parts?

Moon (1999) suggests that the impact of a professional development course is the difference it makes to the participant's practice. She suggests this would be demonstrated in improved or changed behaviour. In the case of the FdA EY, the development of professional and practical skills leads to recognition as a senior practitioner and therefore changes and improvements in professional practice are an expected outcome and a key measure of success. As the mentoring system provides the supportive framework for reflection and skill development, an evaluation of the extent to which it promoted the process of change would also indicate its effectiveness. Bolton (2001) suggests that effective support to others in reflection can increase satisfaction and decrease stress. Increased motivation to effect a change, a sense of liberation to take risks and empowerment to act can result. Some observable or tangible evidence of consequent change in attitudes as well as practice should therefore be apparent as indicators of success. There is potential for a ripple effect of benefits, beyond the individual, arising from enhancement of individual practice as an outcome of effective mentoring. The quality and longevity of changed behaviour are also important considerations for assessing long-term effectiveness and significant impact.

> ## SUCCESS INDICATORS
>
> - Changed behaviour/improved individual practice.
> - Increased satisfaction, motivation, decreased stress.
> - Changed attitudes, empowerment to act and longer-term impact.
> - Impact or influence on others, in the setting and beyond.
> - Sustained quality improvement.

So is it making a difference, to whom, and in what way? An evaluation of the Worcester mentoring scheme is an ongoing process to identify immediate and longer-term impact. Personal stories and perspectives are being collected from participants in the first phase of evaluation. Personal stories provide insights into the experience of mentoring and personal interpretations of its meaning and significance to the individual. In this sense it can be argued that personal stories provide valid 'field-sensitive evidence' (MacNaughton *et al.*, 2001: 124). In the early stages, personal impact is likely to be the major evidence, where mentoring is making a difference to the individual. Feedback from PMs, with a year or eighteen months' involvement (sample 6=85 per cent), rated the outcomes and influence of the mentoring scheme highest in providing individual support and lowest in gaining the involvement of stakeholders, i.e. the employer, the profession and the wider sector. Wider impact through influencing practice in the setting and the sector would not necessarily be an expectation at this stage but any evidence of impact beyond the individual would be an indicator of future potential and encourage positive steps to develop a mentoring culture and foster a wider learning community.

Perspectives and personal stories

Although the evaluation is at an early stage, personal stories from PMs and practitioner-students are beginning to indicate aspects which could affect or contribute to the impact of a mentoring scheme. Broadly, these are:

- Support in the workplace.
- Layers of mentoring support.
- Relationship building.
- Interactions and communication.

Support in the workplace

PMs and practitioners have identified key issues in relation to support in the workplace, in terms of:

- Employers valuing and recognising achievement.
- Opportunities for career enhancement.
- Being open to change and adaptations of practice.
- The dependence on the quality and availability of the PCF.
- The ability to choose the workplace mentor (PCF).

Support in the workplace: recognising achievement/career enhancement

Personal stories – practitioners:

> It would have been hard not to have a mentor. It gave me a lot of support. I felt isolated. There wasn't the understanding in school. It was awkward justifying what I was learning. I am a Level 3 classroom assistant and there is no position for a Level 4. The Head didn't want to raise me above the others. We have a new Head now … . Now I have finished I am more knowledgeable. I have gained personally and professionally but it hasn't been acknowledged … . The Head asked me to go on the Write On project. I was representing the school. I did literature research as part of the course and showed it to the Head. I suppose it shows she is acknowledging what I have done as she asked me to go.

> It hasn't changed my status. It is the same job. There are no openings for the Senior Practitioner but I am hoping it means the Head is acknowledging it more.

Support in the workplace: quality, availability and choice of the PCF

Personal stories – practitioners:

> It is important to choose them [the PCF]. It could have been negative otherwise, if they had not understood. I chose a teacher I could rely on. My PCF felt she didn't support me enough but she didn't realise that by just having her was enough. I could ask when I needed her.

> I chose the duty co-ordinator for the team. She is very professional and non-judgemental. She is also the person I would seek help, support and advice from regarding … any issues or concerns I may have that affect my working practice both personally and/or professionally. For me the choice was easy, as I felt it very important to choose someone that I felt comfortable and confident with and who I knew had a wealth of experience herself.

> Benefits included having her there in the same working environment and involved in the same line of work … Difficulties – none in particular, she always made time to discuss anything with me when I needed to.

Support in the workplace: open to change and adaptations of practice

Personal stories – PMs:

> Many students have been able to implement new ideas within their settings. The settings seem really happy for them to do so. I have seen new ways of planning and recording.

> Where the workplace is open to the increasing knowledge of the student, the student can make a contribution in terms of improving the quality of the practice. One student has been able to help young teachers working in the early years for the first time, another used information gained on a child protection module to work with a parent. Students often use mentor time to discuss new activities and initiatives they have undertaken as part of their professional development.

Where employer involvement is high, adaptations of practice are more likely to occur. Mentoring can encourage and facilitate application of new learning but it is not necessarily the most significant factor in the changes brought about through professional development courses. As one practitioner stated,

> I do not feel that I have changed due to having a mentor but I have changed as a person and professionally since undertaking the FdA EY. This is due to experiencing a higher level of study and appreciating that we are all involved in making a difference to children's lives for the better. I now look and analyse situations differently.

Layers of mentoring support

A tiered system of mentoring provides internal and external guidance which gives strength of support, different levels of support and provides a 'failsafe' element, where practitioners can relate to at least one source of help. For some, it was the combination which was effective:

> I have gone through the traumas. My mentors made me realise it was manageable. I might not have got to the end and was tempted to 'throw in the towel' at times. My mentor helped those times. There was a sense of family and community with the mentor and the college.

For others a particular mentor was the main source of support.

> Personally, the PCF was more beneficial to me, as she was able to offer concrete advice and support in relation to my work and adapting it to fit in with certain assessment criteria.

External mentors provided a different level of expertise and status which guided and affirmed the students' practice and provided a different perspective or source of confidence for discussion and feedback.

Personal stories – practitioners

> I used to look forward to her coming in and enjoyed our discussions …
> They [staff in the setting] were curious why I had a PM coming in to
> observe my practice. If I had not had a mentor coming in it would have
> been blind leading blind, wouldn't it? I think it is important for the mentors
> to see what you are like as a practitioner, which might be different from the
> way you are as a student.

> It enabled me to show the PM my own field of work, skills, knowledge and
> expertise and get positive feedback.

Relationship building

Common themes emerging from the PM feedback suggest that mentoring is
highly dependent on building a trusting relationship which can then empower
risk taking to make a change. This is illustrated by the following extract from a
PM story:

> One particular student has taken on board the idea that she should dele-
> gate more to her staff. It required somebody who knew her setting and her
> current working practice to say this to her and then to encourage further
> reflection on the benefit of doing so.

Effective and trusting relations between mentors and practitioners also led to
increased confidence in the practitioner to apply theory in practice, and
develop professional skills and competences in a supported context, as evidenced by the following extracts:

Personal stories – PMs

> Most practitioners grow in self-confidence as they progress through the
> course. However, many seem to work in difficult situations or ones in which
> they are not valued. They are often moved around the school or to work
> with other children, with no consultation or opportunity to give their profes-
> sional opinion about their work, or say what they would like to do. I have
> worked with students who have really benefited from having a mentor who
> can listen, give positive feedback about their practice, can sympathise with
> their situation and perhaps give some constructive comments. It is particu-
> larly helpful where a second mentor has visited the student and both have
> given similar support.

> I think that the mentor encourages a self-belief in their student that is so
> often lacking in mature students.

Personal stories – practitioner

> I know a lot more now. I feel on a par with the new NQT … I have had a chance to do a nurture group and I have got the confidence now which I wouldn't have had before.

Interactions and communication

Communication between all parties involved in the mentoring process is essential and the PM plays a significant liaison role. A benefit identified by one partner college was the opportunity the mentoring system offered for developing good working relations within the local area, in the local authority and the sector, raising the profile of the college.

The layers of interactions within the mentoring system encourage connections and dialogue within and beyond the system itself, enabling learning to be derived from shared stories and experiences. 'I have also seen a sharing of good practice between the students, and they have implemented things such as "brain gym" . ' (PM). The following extract indicates mutual value to mentor (PCF) and practitioner.

> We found the EYP folders hard to understand and we analysed them together. It benefited her as well, refreshed things in her mind. There were things she knew from before and this brought them back and she said where we could use them now.
>
> (Practitioner)

This is the type of dialogue referred to by Freire, which is more than a conversation and recognises 'the social and not merely the individualistic character of the process of knowing' (Freire and Macedo 1996: 48).

 Points to remember

The key issues to emerge from this chapter are that:

- Mentoring schemes are most likely to be effective where they take account of the unique learning situation. In the early years sector a system based on a fusion of pedagogy and andragogy is most likely to suit the nature of the workplace context and the learner's situation within it.
- Early and sustained involvement of the sector is critical for effective design and implementation of an early years mentoring scheme.

- A tiered mentoring system provides layers of interactions to support shared learning, common channels of communication and liaison, and a blend of formal and informal mentoring support.
- Mentoring recognises the social character of learning and the construction of knowledge and understanding through dialogue.
- Practice-based learning and the role of the mentor need to be overtly recognised and valued through accreditation and training.
- Impact studies are needed to identify the significance of mentoring, and the nature, extent and potential scope for promoting learning and improvement in practice.

📖 Further reading

Knowles, M.S., Holton III, E.F., and Swanson, R.A. (1998). *The Adult Learner* (5th edn). Foley, TX: Gulf Publishing. For developing understanding of andragogy, principles of adult learning.

Moon, J .A. (1999) *Reflection in Learning and Professional Development*. London: RoutledgeFalmer. For further practical guidance and case studies on promoting learning in professional situations.

6

Mentoring the process of change:
a case study
Sarah Kelly

This chapter describes the role of the mentor within a setting and will show how the mentoring process can encourage the development of critical reflective practice and lead to changes and improvements in the quality of educational provision for young children. It is based on personal experience and describes how, as a mentor, I worked with a nursery school team to assess and develop aspects of their practice and provision. The chapter explores the challenges faced when undertaking a mentoring project. It goes on to describe how to support staff to take on new ideas and to integrate them into their practice and make substantial changes and improvements.

A framework for development

For some years I have been involved with mentoring early years practitioners who have used the Effective Early Learning (EEL) programme (Bertram and Pascal, 2004) as a method of developing the quality of their practice and provision. As part of the EEL research team based at the University of Worcester, I have worked as a mentor with early years practitioners in a whole range of settings across the country, initially training them to use the programme to evaluate their current practice and provision and then supporting their development through the cycle of evaluation, action planning, improvement and reflection. The EEL programme began in 1993 as a research project at Worcester College of Higher Education (now the University of Worcester), aiming to evaluate and improve the quality and effectiveness of early learning available to three- and four-year-old children in a wide range of education and care settings. It has since become the largest early childhood evaluation and quality development and assurance programme in the UK. The EEL programme is based on the view that quality improvement takes place through supported self-evaluation using an action research approach. Regular support from an external adviser, or mentor, is normally provided throughout the process, in addition to any support which may be available within the setting.

Action research is a method of implementing change and improvement through a series of repeated steps which include: the evaluation of current practice; planning improvements; carrying them out and observing their effects; and then reflecting on the process and the outcomes. Action research has proved attractive to practitioners and researchers because of its practical focus, its flexibility and adaptability to a range of situations, and its collaborative nature. This collaboration can involve the use of external mentors to support the participants in the improvement process and to engage in critical reflection. The benefits of action research are discussed in more detail in Chapter 3. The EEL programme is a clearly structured model for evaluation, action, development and reflection which encourages the development of critical reflective practice through teamwork and with the support of an external mentor. As well as my role as an EEL external adviser I am a practice mentor for the Foundation Degree in Early Years, working with practitioners at two of the University of Worcester's partner institutions.

Setting the scene

My initial training was as a primary school teacher and when I joined the EEL team I had little experience of working with children younger than those entering reception classes. So I approached my former head teacher, who had recently taken on the headship of an LEA nursery school some distance away. I asked her whether I could work with her to gain some first-hand experience in a nursery school while at the same time using and developing my mentoring skills. She had been appointed to a run-down and poorly resourced nursery school with three nursery nurses who had all been there for over twenty years and she was worried about how to start making changes and develop the practice. She was also keen to encourage the staff to begin working together as a team, which they had not done previously. The staff had worked with four previous head teachers and over the years had developed their own individual routines and organisation which she felt they might find difficult to modify. However, they were all aware that change was necessary and were open to suggestions about where to start, particularly in the light of an impending Ofsted inspection. The mounting pressures at both local and national level to improve and develop provision in line with requirements for statutory schooling had left the staff feeling threatened and with little confidence in themselves or in what they were doing. They felt that they were being bombarded with an array of initiatives which they were expected to implement, but were not always able to see their relevance or indeed how they all fitted together for the benefit of the children. Furthermore at that stage there was limited in-service provision in the county for nursery nurses and there were no local support networks. Following my discussion with the head teacher, the staff and I agreed that I would work with them for one day a week over a six-month period.

As a first step in the process of implementing change and encouraging the staff to work together as a team, the head teacher suggested that she and her staff work together, with myself as mentor, to develop the school's planning, assessment and record-keeping procedures. The staff had highlighted these areas in their School Development Plan as needing to be addressed, so it seemed to be a good starting point. Using aspects of the EEL programme, we began with a review of the existing planning, assessment and record-keeping procedures and discussed ways forward, details of which are described in action–reflection cycle 1. As we started the process it became clear to me that in order to develop this or any other aspect of the practice we needed to take a step back and review the nursery's aims and the underlying principles support-ing those aims. This would ensure that all the staff shared a common vision for the direction of their practice and would provide a basis for all future develop-ment. Having used the EEL programme extensively with early years practitioners for quality development, I felt that it would provide a structure to help the staff take an overall look at their provision and practice, and to focus on ways of developing and improving the quality of the children's educational experiences at the nursery. From my previous experience I also felt that work-ing through this process would be good preparation for their forthcoming Ofsted inspection with its focus on evaluating and developing quality.

Establishing roles and relationships

As a mentor, I knew that I would be able to support the staff through the EEL process, bring an outside perspective, introduce new materials and ideas, and in particular help them to structure the developments so that they would be manageable and relevant. However, within this collaborative model of an exter-nal mentor working alongside the staff, I was also very aware of the importance of the staff themselves taking ownership and control of the process and its out-comes, so that in the longer term they would be able to continue the development process without external support. The staff were very anxious to ensure that all the requirements of the Ofsted inspection process were in place and this, more than anything else, provided the impetus for and the direction of the developmental work which we undertook.

A first step is to understand the needs of the team you are mentoring, so I began working straight away to get to know, and build up relationships with, the staff. I did this in a number of ways. First, during my weekly visits to the school I talked to the head teacher and staff, both individually and as a group, listened to their needs and concerns and attempted to find answers to some of their questions. Second, I had informal but structured discussions with each member of staff. These followed a set of questions looking at their views on early years education, their hopes and aspirations for the nursery, their roles within the nursery – particularly what they enjoyed and what they wished to change, their future career ambitions and the training they would need to achieve them. Although the subjects covered were the same for each member of staff, the discussions were not interviews. I sat next to them and listened and responded rather than simply writing down their answers, although I made notes in my own personal journal so that I would remember conversations accurately, and I reassured them that the purpose of these discussions was to help me build up a picture of the nursery. Third, I worked from time to time in the nursery on a supply basis, which meant that I was able to get to know the children and some of the parents. It is important as a mentor that you are seen to understand the roles of, and problems faced by, the practitioners and I hoped that by working in the setting I would gain credibility.

A challenge faced by mentors is that you can be seen as the 'expert', and it can be daunting to have to provide answers to a whole range of questions and reassurance about the direction the staff should be taking. The staff frequently asked what the 'right' way was, or whether other nurseries were doing the same things as they were. I shared the experiences I had, but also reassured them that there is not necessarily one 'right' way to develop quality. Where questions were technical ones about learning methods or procedures, I would undertake research between weekly meetings and report back on what I had found.

As trusting relationships developed, the staff appreciated the opportunity to talk to me about their concerns while at the same time helping me to understand their roles in the school. The fact that I was building up a link with each member of staff, and already knew the head teacher, made it easier for us to start to talk together about our educational interests and concerns. These began as general staff-room conversations, but became more focused on the nursery and its development. This was an important stage of the team-building process because previously the staff had worked individually and rarely shared ideas and knowledge.

Throughout the process I openly kept notes in my journal of visits, the discussions and the queries and my own reflections which provided me with a record of the developments and changes that were taking place. At the end of the period I used these notes to write an evaluation report for the Ofsted inspection to document the development work that had taken place.

During this initial period I became increasingly aware of differing needs among the staff. Some were more confident than others and more willing to talk about their successes and their worries, or to admit that they did not know or understand something. It was vital to build up an atmosphere of mutual trust so that all the staff felt able to talk openly and I felt that they trusted me, if we were to develop through collaborative team working. As a mentor committed to an open and shared approach I was able to make this process work, as I had the time to spend with staff both individually and as a group. I was supported greatly by the head teacher, who gave staff the opportunity to spend time with me during my visits. The building up of trust and a feeling among the staff that the changes will benefit them takes time to develop. Cohen and Manion (1994: 194) talk of the need for participants to be favourably disposed towards a project in order for action research to be successful: 'it is important, therefore, that teachers taking part in the project are truly involved, that they know what the objectives are, what these imply, and that they are adequately motivated …'.

In my experience, whilst the staff were aware at the outset that they needed to make changes, their involvement grew as the process developed. They became more motivated and confident as they began to see the benefits of the development work. Their confidence in themselves both individually and as a team increasingly enabled them to critically reflect on their practice.

PAUSE FOR THOUGHT

Building an open and trusting relationship as a mentor

- Listen carefully to the ideas and concerns of practitioners and make sure you understand their needs and role in the setting.
- Keep things informal but structured.
- Remember to seek individual opinions as well as those of a group – people may open up more when they are alone.
- Gain credibility by working alongside practitioners.

The process of change

The development phase involved myself and the staff working through three action–reflection cycles of six to eight weeks each, in which we looked at aspects of the practice and provision needing to be addressed. During these cycles we worked through a process of considering possible solutions, implementing those ideas, monitoring, evaluating, reflecting and rethinking on a continuous basis. I led weekly meetings with the head teacher and staff where we reflected on progress so far and planned future actions. The ideas were researched and implemented during the time in between meetings. For the sake of clarity I have described the development work in three separate cycles below, although there was obviously some overlapping between cycles and in some cases the developments could not be wholly implemented within one cycle, but were completed as the staff learned the necessary skills to implement them. As their mentor, my concern throughout the six-month period was to present the new ideas in a way which was acceptable to the staff, and which would help them to see the relevance of different aspects of the EEL programme and how these would all fit together to raise the quality of education at the nursery. This was achieved by focusing on one aspect of development at a time, as I describe in the action–reflection cycles below. The pace and timing were crucial, as we had to work within a limited time scale and we needed to be realistic about what was achievable. Too many changes can be overwhelming and can mean that practitioners are not receptive to new ideas. In order to keep morale up the mentor needs to be adaptable, breaking things down into manageable steps, dropping prepared plans if necessary and listening and responding to the needs of the staff.

Action–reflection cycle 1: planning, assessment and record keeping

Before I arrived the staff had decided they wanted to develop their planning, assessment and record-keeping procedures, and so this was a natural first step. I suggested that a good starting point would be to review what was already happening. This would enable us to identify areas needing to be addressed and to build on existing practice. I asked the staff to describe briefly how they organised each of the three areas, and, having discussed it with them, I drafted a short report of their responses and indicated possible areas for development. These included more consistent planning for the whole nursery, manageable and relevant assessments of children and an accessible and up-to-date record-keeping system.

The planning section of the report listed the range of opportunities, activities and resources provided daily. This highlighted gaps in the provision and gave the staff the impetus to begin to sort and reorganise resources, clear out old equipment from cluttered cupboards and think about alternative uses for equipment. At the same time the head teacher and myself collected examples of good practice in planning, and reflecting on these as a team during the weekly meetings informed the staff of the need to provide a broader and more balanced curriculum. At our weekly meetings we worked together to develop whole-school planning documents covering all aspects of the curriculum. At a later stage the staff were able to focus more specifically on each curriculum area to develop their curriculum policies and used the same method of working together to review, research and then develop practice.

Assessments of children's progress were being made through informal observation and discussion with parents and between staff, and summative assessment lists charted children's achievements. However, these were not always dated, regularly carried out or detailed enough, so it was difficult to see progress, and as one member of staff pointed out during the review, 'They don't give us enough information about individual children, where they were when they started at the nursery and the progress they are making.' The process we were going through was encouraging the staff to reflect on current practice and to come up with answers themselves. They were aware that systematic and focused observations of children are an integral part of good early years practice, both to inform the planning and for assessment purposes, and we agreed that training in the EEL child observation techniques at a later date would provide them with a method to carry these out. These are explained in more detail in action–reflection cycle 3.

The staff wanted to extend the record-keeping system by setting up individual records for each of the children which would be developed throughout their time at the nursery and would provide continuity between home, nursery and school. They suggested the starting point could be an 'All about me' booklet to be produced for parents to fill in with their children before starting at the nursery. The staff felt that this would provide useful information about the child's pre-school experiences, upon which they could build. So while we agreed that developments in both planning and assessment procedures would take place over a longer period, we could start to develop the record-keeping system immediately. The head teacher and myself produced a booklet using ideas from the staff covering what they needed to know about each child. It was given to the staff in draft form for their comments and was amended at their suggestion, to make it more user-friendly. The booklet was piloted with a group of ten parents. They all, without exception, completed the booklet with their child, in some cases adding extra information and photographs and were very positive about its use. These booklets were kept in the classrooms, were available to both the children and their parents and were the first stage in the establishment of individual records.

PAUSE FOR THOUGHT

Getting involved

- When mentoring a group, it is crucial to involve all members of the group.

- Make sure people can achieve small changes quickly to keep motivation high.

- Introduce big changes over a longer term in small steps.

- Guide people – don't force them.

The implications for the next action–reflection cycle were positive because, as a result of the booklet's success, the staff felt they could see a purpose for further developments in the record-keeping system. The focus on planning and assessment had raised a number of issues about how and why the staff planned and assessed in the way they did, and how these areas might be developed. For example, they could see the need to broaden children's experience in their planning, make more use of the outdoor environment and use more focused observations for their assessments. However, questions had also arisen that were more difficult to resolve because there was confusion about the 'right' way to proceed. These included questions about the way sessions were organised to allow adults more time to interact with children in small groups and individually, time for children to pursue their own interests and the purpose of developing children's autonomy.

From my perspective as mentor, I felt that it was crucial to review the aims and objectives of the nursery school as the next step. This would give us a foundation on which to build, and would also provide answers to some of these questions. However, the staff felt that there were more pressing needs, such as the updating of curriculum policies and other necessary documentation. I felt it important to persuade them that reviewing the aims would be a good use of their time and that it would provide a direction for their work. Although they were not totally convinced at that stage, they did agree to spend part of their weekly meeting time on this with my support. It was only in discussing the process with the head teacher at a later date that she admitted that she had found this step difficult. 'The hardest thing for me was to find a starting point for our development, I had a different starting point from you.'

Action–reflection cycle 2: formulating written aims and objectives

The staff needed to ensure that there was agreement about their aims and beliefs for the education of young children, and understanding of the principles underlying these aims, in order to move forward as a team and develop the quality of their practice. Although individual views gathered from the staff interviews showed a broad consensus of beliefs about the needs of young children and the purposes of nursery education, they had never been involved in formally considering the aims and objectives of the school as a team. As David (1990: 90) says:

> Perhaps the most important issue in any curriculum development is the need for all members of staff to engage in discussion about their underpinning philosophy – what they believe early education is for, how children learn and develop, what their own and parents' roles should be and implications for practice.

We approached the second cycle in the same way as the first, by gathering the views of the staff and then developing and refining them through discussion and reflection at our weekly meetings, and through reference to relevant documentation. The head teacher and myself then drafted the aims and objectives and gave them to the staff for their comments and amendments before the final version was written. Working together on this document, the staff began to understand the benefits of having shared aims related to their practice. This encouraged them to develop the nursery aims into a working document which included the early years principles (from the *Curriculum Guidance for the Foundation Stage*, DfES, 2000). The abstract aims were followed by examples, references and photographs of the way in which each of them was being carried out in practice. This document, because of time constraints, was developed over a longer period of time, alongside the updating of curriculum and other policies. Over that time they were adopted by the staff team themselves, who were becoming increasingly confident in working together without my support.

The discussions and the resulting aims document had highlighted aspects of practice which were very positive, working well or being developed, and as mentor I felt it was very important to acknowledge these successes and for the staff to feel a sense of satisfaction. For example, the school had an excellent reputation for its friendly, supportive and welcoming approach to children and parents, and partnerships were being further developed through a new Family Learning Initiative. The staff were in unanimous agreement about the holistic needs of young children and the direction in which they wanted to develop their practice. Through discussing and acknowledging success the staff felt more positive about their work. They greeted me enthusiastically and always had questions to ask. Importantly, they became more willing to discuss issues as a team and to talk about their difficulties. The head teacher agreed that there was a discernible change in attitude, and I made a note at the time:

All the staff are becoming more open and willing to discuss issues about the nursery, and especially to be open about 'not knowing, not understanding' in front of the rest of the group. This has developed quite markedly and I think is very positive as it helps us to work through problems and queries as a group. There is definitely a more 'democratic' feel to the nursery with everyone seemingly involved and open to the development.

(My journal entry)

From a mentor's viewpoint this was very positive, as it showed the staff taking ownership, reflecting on their practice and working through problems and developments as a team.

PAUSE FOR THOUGHT

Building a team

- Listen to the thoughts and concerns of all practitioners, and spend time having group discussions on key issues.

- Be open to ideas.

- Ensure that new ideas are discussed and agreed – not just implemented without warning.

- Acknowledge success and build the confidence of practitioners.

Action–reflection cycle 3: training in and implementing the EEL observation techniques leading to developments in many aspects of the practice

The discussion that was developing out of the action–reflection cycles and the writing of the nursery aims had highlighted a number of areas which the staff wanted to address. Most importantly, the need for systematic methods of observing the children had arisen in action–reflection cycle 1. Regular observation would enable the staff to plan more appropriately for individual children. I hoped that, by using the EEL observation scales, we could find a workable method of ongoing assessment which could be used for individual children's records. The staff also wanted to consider the balance and range of activities and opportunities as they developed the curriculum policies, and how to encourage children's concentration and involvement in activities. They wanted to look more closely at the adult's role in the learning process, to extend children's learning through increased and relevant adult–child interactions and to provide more opportunities for the development of children's autonomy. The EEL child and adult observation scales would provide the staff with information to address all these points.

Using the EEL training videos, I trained the staff in each of the observation techniques. Much of the discussion that followed was ongoing at the weekly staff meetings or while I was helping in the nursery. We did not have time to complete the adult observations at that stage, but the training and discussion had raised awareness of the crucial role of the adult in the learning process and ways in which the staff could develop the quality of their interactions. The child observations were managed by setting up a clear timetable of observation times and observers, organised so that all the staff, including the head teacher, had the chance to observe the same range of children. The EEL programme uses two methods of observing children. The Child Involvement Scale measures the level of a child's involvement in an activity in the belief that high levels of involvement lead to deep-level learning. Child Tracking focuses on the context in which young children learn: on the child's learning experiences, degree of choice, level of interactions and how children are grouped.

When they were complete the results were drawn up as graphs by the whole team and reflected on together. This process, more than anything, drew the staff together as a unified team, particularly as they found the concept of 'Involvement' a new and fascinating way of looking at children's learning. As one member of staff said, 'Once you have used the scale you can never look at a child again without giving him a level and ... [then] you start to think how you can increase that level.'

The two child observation techniques provided the staff with manageable methods of observing children but, more importantly, showed them the value of close and systematic observations for assessment and record keeping, and provided information which they were able to use to inform their planning. The planning was developing as the staff kept returning to review and refine it in the light of changes and developments that were being made. Undertaking the observations had consolidated the process of team development by giving the staff practical opportunities to work together and to reflect critically on their findings. The information drawn from the observations was used to improve and develop many aspects of the provision and practice.

Outcomes

The process undertaken provided the following key outcomes for the staff team:

- Increased team work, staff involvement and confidence, encouraging and developing critical reflective practice which was used to promote change and develop the quality of many aspects of the provision.
- Improved planning, assessment and record keeping, with increased parental involvement.
- The development of shared written aims and objectives, curriculum and other policies.
- Training for all staff in the EEL observation techniques, leading to close and systematic child observations which fed back into the planning, assessment and record-keeping procedures.

Having worked with the staff for six months, I wrote a report of the developments that had taken place so far, using the EEL Evaluation Report format. This report described current practice, changes that had been made and how they had been carried out, and plans for further development. It was intended as an interim report for the staff to use for their Ofsted inspection, due at the end of the term. The staff still had areas which they wanted to address. First, they had not yet carried out the adult observations, which they saw as an important way of evaluating their practice. Second, as part of their developing partnership with parents, they planned to seek the views of both the parents and the children on the quality of the provision. Third, they wanted to repeat the observation scales at a later date to give another assessment of the development that had taken place. These developments would take time and evolve as the staff continued to make changes and improvements in the nursery.

How effective was the process from my perspective as a mentor?

I decided to evaluate this model of mentor working alongside practitioners to develop and improve quality in four ways.

1. Improvements in the quality of provision for the children

Having developed overall aims for the nursery school, the staff were able to focus on specific aspects of practice and provision, and changes began to take place in terms of organisation, equipment and resources. The focused weekly discussions gave the staff and myself the opportunity to reflect on each step. Once this cycle of evaluation and improvement had been established, the staff were able to see how they could continue to develop aspects of the practice and provision. The evaluation report gave a clear written summary of the developments that had taken place over the six months.

The Ofsted inspection report was very positive and confirmed for the staff and myself that the development process had been effective. It provided an objective assessment of the quality of the current provision and practice at the nursery school. There were no issues for action, other than two addressed to the local authority concerning fire safety. The staff felt that this was a tremendous achievement, particularly as it was the only school in the area not to fail its inspection. As mentor I felt that the following statement from the inspection report confirmed the fundamental importance of having had clear aims and values as a starting point for the developmental process: 'The aims, values and policies of the school are evident throughout its work. The aims were produced collectively by the staff and permeate the life of the school.' This emphasises the value of having an external mentor who can guide the thinking of the staff, rather than simply responding to immediate pressures.

Observing the involvement of the children in their activity

2. The effect of the process on the professional development of the staff

At the time the project began, the mounting pressure to develop nursery provision together with the lack of in-service training had left the staff, as in many other local nursery settings, feeling threatened and lacking in professional confidence. As the project progressed, the individual and group discussions gave an ongoing indication of the effectiveness of the process on the professional development of the staff. As they were beginning to see the benefits they became more open, willing to ask questions and more reflective about their practice. Throughout the action–reflection cycles the staff were growing increasingly confident in themselves as practitioners and they were noticeably more willing to adapt to the changes taking place. Two of the nursery nurses embarked on further education courses, one a part-time B.Ed. and the other an Advanced Diploma in Care and Education, and this further supported their professional development. The head teacher was encouraged that the staff were committing time for their development and were able to support and encourage each other as they continued to develop aspects of the provision. The positive experience of the Ofsted inspection and the resulting recognition from the local community and from the LEA, together with their growing confidence, gave the staff a feeling of empowerment and professional competence, upon which they were then able to build. As well as keeping up their links with me, one of the staff was asked to move to and support another nursery setting wanting to make changes, so in effect became a mentor herself.

3. My own professional development

In terms of my own professional development, my initial role of helping the nursery staff to develop one aspect of their practice developed into one of supporting and mentoring them through a process of change and development, and of managing the change so that it was accessible and meaningful for them. This involved building up an atmosphere of mutual trust between myself and the staff, and also among the staff team. The pace and timing were crucial, I had to be sensitive about other pressures on the staff, sometimes abandoning my plans for the week, while at the same time keeping up the momentum so that the benefits became evident and the development work was completed sufficiently for the Ofsted inspection. As a mentor I was viewed as the 'expert' who could give answers to a whole range of questions about nursery education. This often meant that I had to go away and undertake research in order to answer the questions and find material to support the development. I think I learned as much from the staff and from their willingness to accept me as a member of their team as they learnt from me. Collaborative action research cannot be effective unless both sides are willing to be open, to learn and to be reflective together, and these are important strategies for implementing development and change.

4. The process as a template for development in other settings

The collaborative action research approach using the EEL framework and methodology was an extremely effective method of implementing change within the nursery school. The researcher–practitioner collaboration described by Aspland *et al.* (1996: 94) in which the practitioner 'brings the perspectives of practice to the research, while the university researcher [mentor] contributes theoretical perspectives which provide ways of critically reflecting on, and transforming practice' resulted in a range of improvements. Mentoring does not have to be at an individual level; it can be equally effective in a team setting.

This method of quality development with weekly support from a mentor over a prolonged period is labour-intensive and perhaps not cost-effective on a general basis. However, where there is a need, and where resources permit, having a mentor closely supporting individuals and small groups of settings can be a very effective method of quality development. As the head teacher at the nursery school suggested, more focused and regular support for small groups of settings with similar needs would be a better use of LEA resources than 'endless in-service training courses aimed at no one in particular'. She believes that the mentor 'needs to understand your starting point and then make links for you'. They need to be 'someone you can trust and who can give you confidence because they've tuned in at the right place'. By working in this way, the mentor can encourage the group to collaborate in critical reflection and to achieve change. This approach is increasingly being recognised as an effective method of in-service training.

Points to remember

This chapter has described the practical process of mentoring in an early years setting.

- Mentor–practitioner collaboration enabled us to develop and improve many aspects of the practice and provision in a nursery school.
- The process also had an impact on the professional development of the adults.
- As the project progressed the staff became open and adaptable to the changes taking place, motivated to work together as a team and increasingly confident in their ability as early childhood educators.
- The collaborative approach encouraged and enabled both the staff and mentor to become more critically reflective as practitioners, an approach which is increasingly being seen as vital to future educational practice.

Further reading/information

More information about the EEL observation scales can be obtained from the Centre for Research in Early Childhood, St Thomas Centre, Bell Barn Road, Birmingham B15 2AF.

Glossary

Action–reflection cycle Applying reflective practice as an ongoing and cyclical process.

Andragogy The science and principles of teaching adults based on the characteristics of adult learners.

Course provider College or training organisation delivering a course.

Criteria Requirements or standards by which learning may be judged.

Critical reflective practice Conscious awareness of thoughts, beliefs, habits and actions which inform our lives and practices, leading to self-evaluation and review.

Dialogue An exchange of view; it can be verbal or written.

Diary A book/journal/log containing details of significant events and experiences with critical evaluations and reflections.

Early Years Profile (EYP) Framework for recording, monitoring and assessing personal, professional and practical skills as part of the UW FdA EY.

Evidence Sample piece of work contained within a profile/portfolio.

Experiential Based on life experiences and situations.

Journal See Diary.

Learning community A group or association of people with common ownership, and enjoyment of the development of learning.

Learning outcomes A set of statements which measure the extent to which knowledge has been learnt and understood.

Log See Diary.

Mentor An experienced and trusted adviser, someone who works or who has worked in the field of early years and is able to offer advice and support.

Mentor(ing) contract The written/spoken agreement between the mentor and the practitioner which ensures that both parties work professionally, with a shared understanding and purpose and within set guidelines.

Partner college/Institution Further education college delivering higher education courses validated by a university.

Pedagogy The science and principles of teaching children based on the characteristics of children as learners.

Perspective transformation New ways of understanding, thinking and analysing, brought about through applying insights from self-examination and reflection.

Portfolio A sample of a practitioner's work contained within a folder. The work is usually organised according to specific standards/criteria/learning outcomes and appropriately annotated by the practitioner as part of their critical reflection.

Practice mentor A professional person who visits a practitioner at their place of work to support, observe, discuss and assess their practice.

Practitioner A person practising a profession, in this case a person working within the field of early years.

Professional critical friend A person, usually in a more senior position within the practitioner's place of work, who is willing to offer informal peer support, guidance and positive, constructive criticism where appropriate.

Profile Another term for a portfolio.

Reflective practice The art of analysing what has been, how it was done and why it was done in that way. This analysis is used to inform future practice.

Senior practitioner The title awarded to graduates of the SureStart-recognised Sector-endorsed Foundation degree in early years.

Stakeholder Any party who has a vested interest in the outcome of a situation (for example, the local authority, school, nursery, parent, carer or child).

Standards The degree of excellence required for a particular course or profession (for example, NVQ and teacher training courses assessed in relation to set standards).

SureStart-recognised, Sector-endorsed Foundation Degree in Early Years (FdA EY) DfES-approved foundation degree. Professional qualification based on a Statement of Requirement for professional and practical skills, for practitioners with a minimum of two years' experience in early years.

References

Aspland, T., MacPherson, I., Proudfoot, C. and Whitmore, L. (1996) 'Critical collaboration action research as a means of curriculum inquiry and empowerment', *Educational Action Research* 4 (1), 93–104

Atkinson, T. and Claxton, G. (eds) (2000) *The Intuitive Practitioner: on the value of not always knowing what one is doing*. Buckingham: Open University Press

Bertram, A. and Pascal, C. (2004) *Effective Early Learning Programme*. Worcester: Amber Publications

Blenkin, G.M. and Kelly, A.V. (1997) *Principles into Practice in Early Childhood Education*. London: Paul Chapman Publishing

Bolton, G. (2001) *Reflective Practice: writing and professional development*. London: Paul Chapman Publishing

Boud, D., Keough, R. and Walker, D. (eds) (1985) *Reflection: turning experience into learning*. London: Kogan Page

Brookfield, S.D. (1995) *Developing Critical Thinkers: challenging adults to explore alternative ways of thinking and acting*. Buckingham: Open University Press

Brown, S. (2000) 'Assessing practice', in S. Brown and A. Glasner (eds) (2000) *Assessment Matters in Higher Education*. Bury St Edmunds: Society for Research into Education

Clutterbuck, D. (2004) *Everyone Needs a Mentor: fostering talent in your organization* (4th edn). London: Chartered Institute of Personnel and Development

Cohen, L. and Manion, L. (1994) *Research Methods in Education* (4th edn). London: Routledge

David, T. (1990) *Under Five – Under-educated?* Buckingham: Open University Press

Dewey, J. (1933) *How we Think: a reinstatement of the relation of reflective Thinking to the Educative Process*. Chicago, IL: Henry Regner Publishers

DfES (1997) *National Childcare Strategy*. London: DfES Publications

DfES (2000) *Curriculum Guidance for the Foundation Stage.* Sudbury: QCA Publications

DfES (2001) *Statement of Requirement for the Early Years Sector-Endorsed Foundation Degree.* London: DfES Publications

DfES (2002) *Effective Provision of Pre-school Education: research brief.* London: DfES Publications

DfES (2003) *Every Child Matters* (summary). London: DfES Publications

DfES (2004) *Every Child Matters: next steps.* London: DfES Publications

DfES (2005) *Common Core of Skills and Knowledge for the Children's Workforce.* London: DfES Publications

DfES (2006) *Children's Workforce Strategy: building a world-class workforce for Children, Young people and Families* (response to consultation). London: DfES Publications

Drury, R., Miller, L. and Campbell, R. (eds) (2000) *Looking at Early Years Education and Care.* London: David Fulton

Dryden, L., Forbes, R., Mukherji, P. and Pound, L. (eds) (2005) *Essential Early Years.* London: HodderArnold

Fowler, K. and Russel, V. (1998) *Portfolios and Professional Development Profiles: approaches to monitoring and assessing PGCE students' progress* (unpublished)

Freire, P. and Macedo, D. (1996) *Pedagogy, Culture, Language and Race: a dialogue.* London: Sage

Fry, H., Ketteridge, S. and Marshall, S. (1999) *A Handbook for Teaching and Learning in Higher Education.* London: Kogan Page

Furlong, J. and Maynard, T. (1995) *The Growth of Professional Knowledge: mentoring student teachers.* London: Routledge

Gardiner, C. (2003) 'Mentoring: towards a professional friendship', in C.M. Downie and P. Basford (eds) *Mentoring in Practice: A Reader.* London: University of Greenwich

Ghaye, A.,and Ghaye, K. (1998) *Teaching and Learning through Critical Reflective Practice.* London: David Fulton

Ghaye, A., Cuthbert, S., Danai, K. and Dennis, D. (1996) *Learning through Critical Reflective Practice I: professional values.* Newcastle upon Tyne: Formword

Hamilton, R. (1993) *Mentoring.* London: Industrial Society

Handy, C. (1993) *The Age of Unreason.* London: Business Books

Knowles, M.S., Holton, E.F. and Swanson, R.A. (1998) *The Adult Learner* (5th edn). Foley, TX: Gulf Publishing

Leeson, C. (2004) 'In praise of reflective practice', in J. Willan, R. Parker-Rees, and J. Savage (eds) *Early Childhood Studies.* Exeter: Learning Matters

MacNaughton, G. (2003) *Shaping Early Childhood: Learners, Curriculum and Context.* Maidenhead: Open University Press

MacNaughton, G., Rolfe, S.A. and Siraj-Blatchford, I. (2001) *Doing Early Childhood Research.* Buckingham: Open University Press

Moon, J.A. (1999) *Reflection in Learning and Professional Development.* London: RoutledgeFalmer

Neale, D. (2005) How the mentor/mentee relationship can have an impact on Quality Provision in Early Years Settings (unpublished Postgraduate Certificate assignment). Worcester: University of Worcester

Nutbrown, C. (1994) *Threads of Thinking: Young Children learning and the Role of Early Education*. London: Paul Chapman Publishing

Parsloe, E. and Wray, M. (2000) *Coaching and Mentoring: practical methods to improve learning*. London: Kogan Page

Pegg, M (2000) *The Art of Mentoring*. Gloucester: Management Books

Penn, H. (1994) 'Working in conflict: developing a dynamic model of equality', in P. Moss and A.R. Pense (eds) (1994) *Valuing Quality in Early Childhood Services: new approaches to defining quality*. London: Paul Chapman Publishing

Pollard, A. and Tann, S. (1994) *Reflective Teaching in the Primary School*. London: Cassell

Potter, C.A. and Richardson, H.L. (1999) 'Facilitating classroom assistants' professional reflection through video workshops', *British Journal of Special Education* 26 (1), 34–6

Robins, A., Ashbaker, B.Y., Enriquez, J. and Morgan, J. (2004) 'Learning to reflect: professional practice for professionals and paraprofessionals'. *Proceedings of the Tenth International Literacy and Education Research Network Conference*, April, pp. 1–10

Smith, P. and West-Burnham, J. (eds) (1993) *Mentoring in the Effective School*. Harlow: Longman

Stephens, P. (1996) *Essential Mentoring Skills: a practical handbook for school-based teacher educators*. Cheltenham: Stanley Thornes

Stephenson, M. and Lehmann, T. (1995) 'Managing change: towards a new paradigm?' in D. Thomas (ed.) (1995). *Flexible Learning Strategies in Higher and Further Education*. London: Cassell

Teachernet (2006) www.teachernet.gov.uk/docbank (accessed 12 March 2006)

Vance, C.N. (1979) 'Women leaders: modern day heroines or societal deviants?', *Image: Journal of Nursing Scholarship* 11 (2), 40–1

Vygotsky, L.S. (1978) *Mind in Society*. Cambridge MA: Harvard University Press

Wilkin, M. (ed) (1992) *Mentoring in Schools*. London: Kogan Page

Winter, R., Buck, A. and Sobiechowska, P. (1999) *Professional Experience and the Investigative Imagination: the art of reflective writing*. London: Routledge

Zachary, L (2000) *The Mentor's Guide*. San Francisco, CA: Jossey-Bass

Index